PRIDE AGAINST PREJUDICE

*Reminiscences of
a Tasmanian Aborigine*

This book contains the essence of the kind of humanity which made this island a human place

for Ida

ERIC WILLMOT
Principal
Australian Institute of Aboriginal Studies

Aunt Ida's book will bring warmth, humour and sometimes sadness to the reader. Each chapter has a personal meaning and impact that not only her own people will relate to, but that all people should acknowledge. The love and respect that Aunt Ida has gained in the community and her sincerity is felt in this book. Hopefully, it will be appreciated.

GREG DICKSON
Friend

PRIDE AGAINST PREJUDICE

Reminiscences of a Tasmanian Aborigine

Ida West

Australian Institute of
Aboriginal Studies
Canberra 1984

Published in Australia by the
Australian Institute of Aboriginal Studies,
GPO Box 553, Canberra, ACT 2601.

Sold and distributed in North and South America by
Humanities Press Inc.,
171 First Avenue, Atlantic Highlands, NJ 07716.
USA edition ISBN 0 391 03126 0.

The views expressed in this publication are those of the
author and not necessarily those of the Australian
Institute of Aboriginal Studies.

© Ida West 1984. Apart from any fair dealing for the
purpose of private study, research, criticism or review, as
permitted under the Copyright Act, no part of this
publication may be reproduced by any process
whatsoever without the written permission of the
publisher.

AIAS new series no. 51.

National Library of Australia
Cataloguing in Publication data:

> West, Ida, 1919–
> Pride against prejudice.
> ISBN 0 85575 155 X.
>
> [1]. Aborigines, Tasmanian—Social life and
> customs.
> 2. Flinders Island (Tas.)—Social life and customs.
> I. Australian Institute of Aboriginal Studies. II.
> Title.
>
> 994'.0049915

Typeset at Griffin Press Limited, Netley, South Australia.
Printed in Australia by Southwood Press Pty Ltd, Sydney.

84.8.1000

Foreword

The history of Tasmanian Aborigines is one of horror. From first contact by white man, Tasmanian Aboriginal people have been systematically, and in a cold blooded manner, culturally savaged. A direct result of this systematic genocide is the present major struggle of my people, a constant and never ending fight for recognition of our Aboriginality—a legacy of colonial days which is divested on both the descendants of the traditional owners of Tasmania and the descendants of the Empire which dispossessed my people.

Very few Aboriginal people have written about their personal and national history and this work, because of its very personal nature, is a forerunner for Tasmanian Aborigines.

Mrs Ida West holds a position within the Tasmanian Aboriginal communities as a traditional elder, hence her history is of vital importance both spiritually and genealogically. As a tribute to Aunty Ida and the spirit of Aboriginal survival and growth, the following verses are written to elicit the true spirit of this most important Aboriginal History.

There is no-one to teach me the songs that bring the Moon Bird, the fish or any other thing that makes me what I am.
No old women to mend my spirit by preaching my culture to me—
No old man with the knowledge to paint my being.
The spectre of the past is what dwells within—
I search my memory of early days to try to make my presence real, significant, whole.

I use my childhood memories of places, people and words to re-create my identity.
Uncle Leedham, a fine black man is my fondest memory—
He could sing, he could dance and play the mouth organ or gum leaf.

His broad shoulders carried me and, as I remember, I found it a great pleasure.

I owe him and his contemporaries a debt—and I'll pay—
But there is no-one to teach me the songs that bring the Moon
    Bird, the fish or any other thing that makes me what I am.

Like dust blown across the plain are the people of the Moon
    Bird—
Whitey said, 'You'll be better over there, you will grow again!'

Oh, how wrong he was—why the graves of children run four
    deep—all victims of a foreign disease.

They had no resistance to the legacy of the white invasion—or so
    they must have thought
I am their legacy and I'll not disgrace them,
But there is no-one to teach me the songs that bring the Moon
    Bird, the fish or any other thing that makes me what I am.

Inside, a warrior of ages rises up—my soul he possesses, his
    righteous indignation is the cup from which I drink—
I do not want blood—just opportunity—to be,
But even with him within there is no-one to teach me the songs
    that bring the Moon Bird, the fish or any other thing that
    makes me what I am.

Though wretched the invaders were—for me they created a
    greater wretchedness for they, at least, spoke their language,
    understood their role, yet it was nothing to be sought.

My great-grandparents knew their culture and it could not be
    taken from them,
Through the minutes since their life it was taken from me—though
    my warrior within says differently—
Even yet there is no-one to teach me the songs that bring the
    Moon Bird, the fish or any other thing that makes me what I
    am.

ERROL WEST

Contents

Foreword   by Errol West   *page v*

Acknowledgments   *page viii*

Preface   Why I decided to write this book   *page 1*

Chapter one   The early days   *page 3*

Chapter two   The middle years   *page 27*

Chapter three   Memories   *page 43*

Chapter four   Songs and sadness   *page 73*

Chapter five   Nowadays   *page 85*

Appendix one   Verse by Auntie Sarah Mansell   *page 97*

Appendix two   Extracts from *The Last of the Tasmanians* by James Bonwick and references to William Lanne   *page 99*

Acknowledgments

I am most grateful to so many people for all their help and encouragement in writing this book. I would like to thank Verna Nichols, Girlie and Tim Purdon, Kay Price, Anne Reynolds, the late Gussie Maynard, Cheryl Brown, Roy Nichols Jr., Greg Nichols, Andrew Nichols, Molly Mallett, the late Keith and Ena Everett, Alma Stackhouse, Lois Farley, Phyllis Pitchford, Paul White, Mark West, Auntie Sarah Mansell, Darcy and the late Gladys Maynard, Patsy Cameron, Ben and Nellie Everett, Auntie Isobelle Everett, Graham Holloway, Robbie Page, Erroll West, Greg Dickson, Stephen Murray-Smith, Andrew Reynolds, Mr Plomley, Lee Prince of the Tasmanian Arts Advisory Board and the Principal and staff of the Institute of Aboriginal Studies in Canberra.

As help and information came from so many people it is hard to remember all the names, but I wish to thank everyone concerned. To my daughter, Lenna, and son, Darrell, a special thanks, for this book is for them and for my family and grandchildren, and the Aboriginal people of Tasmania and Bass Strait Islands.

Preface

WHY I DECIDED TO WRITE THIS BOOK

We have had Europeans writing about us for years. As a child I can remember people writing about us, they called us half-castes then, they might just as well have called us outcasts.

The newspaper *Truth* went over to Cape Barren Island and wrote a story on the half-castes. They said, 'The sins of their Fathers still drag them down'.

The late Mr Dyer went over to Cape Barren and said the half-castes were 'human driftwood'.

The late Miss Ada Hudson put a story in the *Mercury* newspaper about oranges for half-castes. My son was going to Albuera Street Primary School at the time and he came home and told me that Miss Hudson said he was to get oranges. When I saw the big letters stating 'Oranges for half-castes', I told him that he couldn't take them. I went out and bought some oranges myself. I knew that Miss Hudson meant well, but I still had my pride.

We were brought up to respect our European relations but to be ashamed of Aboriginal relations, though from what I have seen in books the Europeans haven't been too good either. If everyone looked at home first they wouldn't have room to talk about other people. It doesn't matter what race you are.

It has taken me years to complete this book. I have never done anyone any harm. I mixed with everyone, tried to help people of all colours and races, as some have helped me. It was my sister Girlie, niece Leonie, daughter Lenna, daughter-in-law Elizabeth and cousin Clyde Mansell who told me to continue scribbling. I would stick the notes in a drawer on the shelf where they lay almost forgotten.

One night while watching television I saw a Legal Aid person for my people talking to someone about what the Europeans did to Aborigines, cutting their heads off and so on. He pulled out a drawer filled with Aboriginal heads all shapes and sizes, and the sight of the skulls started to turn my stomach. The second drawer was full also. By the third drawer I felt faint. The Legal Aid person said, 'Would you like to have your grandfather's head in there?'

So I got back to the book and kept writing.

One Saturday morning a dear friend came to see me, to give me money to put on a horse race, before the Melbourne Cup. (I chose Lelanie with Roy Higgins on her back). When she went to the door to go home I was behind her. This lady said, 'Ida, you're getting shot at!' I was looking down a gun barrel. I fell back in the door. My friend got away. I was trembling all over. I peeped through the window, the man turned and walked up the street. I knew that the gun wasn't to be fired. After talking to the police, I found out that this man had bouts of depression. After watching a show on television about Aborigines he must have decided that because he knew I was an Aborigine he would do something about it. I was going to press charges, but because of my friend's poor eyesight and age we thought that they may not take her word for it, so I decided not to. Had he pulled the trigger I would not be alive today. Someone else would have had to write this book.

Chapter one
The early days

CHILDHOOD, 1925

My father moved about a lot because of his work. We never settled in the one place until Dad bought the land at Killiecrankie, in the far north of Flinders Island, where our Armstrong forebears had been settled for generations. My brother, Owen, was born at Launceston, Esme was born at Pinescrub at West End on the northwest of Flinders Island, Ila (Girlie) on the Reserve on Cape Barren Island, and my youngest sister Bernice at Lughrata on Flinders Island (in a haunted house which had been brought over from Goose Island). I was born on the Reserve at Cape Barren Island on 30 September 1919, the second daughter of the late Ivy Victoria Albeana (Everett) and Henry Isaac Armstrong. I was delivered by the late Mrs Julie Burgess, a famous island midwife.

We lived at Killiecrankie for a time before I started school, and never saw anyone except our relations. At one time a fishing boat called the *Rachel Thompson* ran up on the beach. Two fishermen, a Mr Nolan and his mate, were aboard; they didn't have any food, so they came up to the house. After a cup of tea and a meal Dad helped them float the boat. We children heard strange voices and hid under the bed. We wouldn't come out to shake hands, and didn't move until the men went away. When we were in our teens

My grandmother Mrs Ida Armstrong (nee Beeton) as a young woman.

we met the fishermen and their sons and finally shook hands.

It was about this time Mum and Dad decided to move to Howell's, a bungalow at Lughrata where we could go to school and meet people. Up until then we only saw Uncle Bun, Charlie Jones, Uncle Johnny Smith and Gran' Aunt Millie (wife of Johnny Smith). All Gran' Aunt Millie's children died, so she took in Athol and Sid Howard and reared them with Charlie Jones. Gran' Aunt Millie also reared another boy called King (or Wright), and also Maria—all these children with the exception of Maria were white. Charlie Jones was an amazing man, he was triple-jointed, there was a doctor who wanted his body when he died. He wanted to pay Charlie 300 pounds and we said to Charlie, you had better take it now because they will probably take you just the same.

SCHOOL

When I was six or seven years old, I went to school at Lughrata three days a week. We had to walk four miles each way from Howell's, and sometimes I would cry all the way home because my flannels (I was prone to bronchitis) chafed me.

There were no more than thirty to forty children attending the school. We had a lot of different teachers, but Miss Dolly Barry was the one I remember the best. She was very staid, and made me use my right hand although I was naturally left-handed.

A lady and her three children who came from England came up and lived near Howell's. The first day at school we met up with her children, and seven of us all walked home together.

Mum would walk down to wait and meet us after school. She would wait where the road turned off to go up to where this English lady lived. This lady was coming down the road to meet her children, but when she saw my mother she turned around and ran back up the hill. We asked Mum what she was running away from, Mum thought about it and said, 'I know'. Mum sang out to this lady, 'Stop at once', and she said it with authority. The lady stopped. Mum walked up to her. The woman was very frightened. Mum asked her why she had run away. Mum said she knew why, but she wanted the lady to tell her. The lady told her that she was frightened of us and said that she was told that black people would

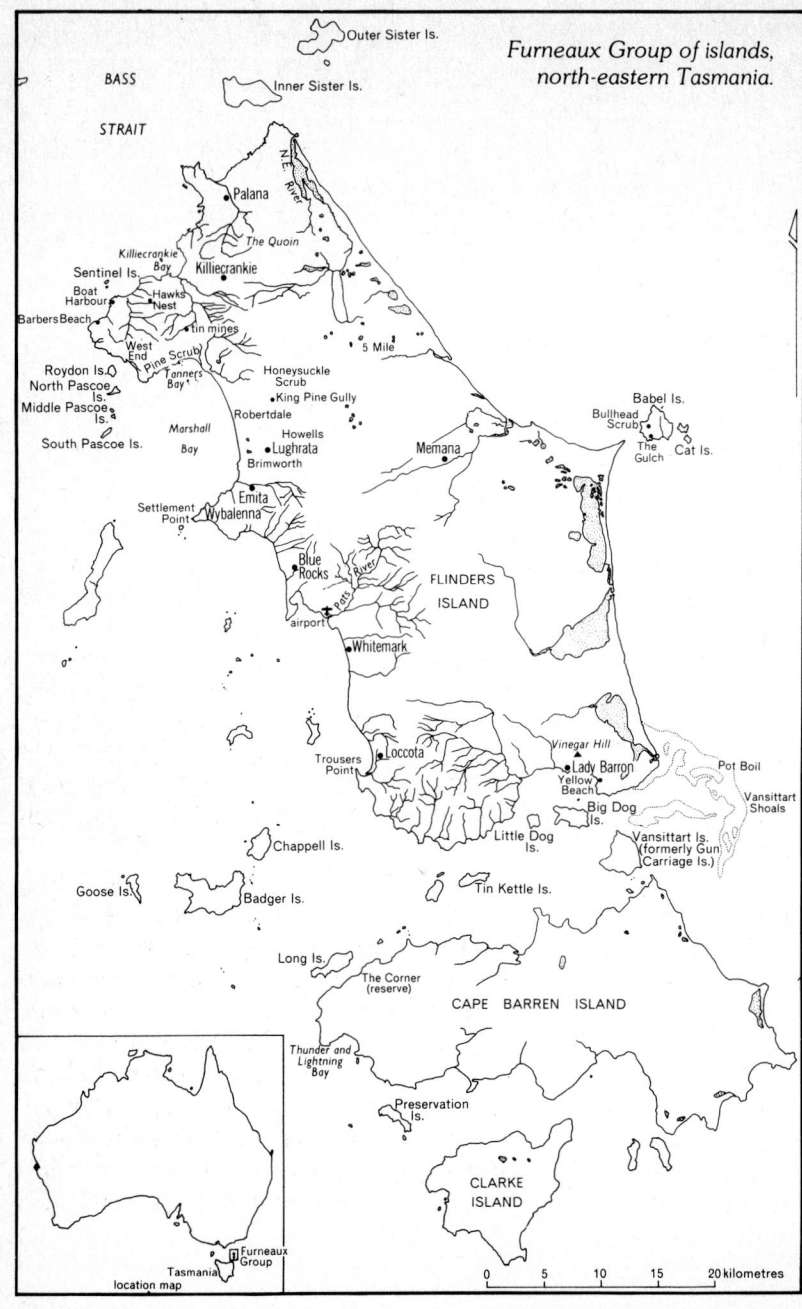

eat her or kill her when she arrived on Flinders Island. The lady didn't say who had told her that.

The Tasmanian Education Department would send teachers over to Flinders Island, where they would stay for about six or twelve months, sometimes longer. Some of the teachers I remember were: Mr Anderson, Mr Colin Thorn, Mr George Fish, Mr Lindsay Best, Mr Claude Glover, Miss Arnott, Mr Mick Dwyer, Mr Ronald Points, Mr Hugo Gottolile, Mr and Mrs Langton.

Each November a sports day was held for all children, and every child had to participate. All the Island schools would enter, and at that time there were five: Lughrata School, Blue Rocks School, Whitemark School, Lady Barron School, and Lacotta School. The prizes were Australian Flags—we were so proud to bring our flag back. There were no trophies to be won, we had a lollie scramble instead.

One day all the children were chasing my sister Girlie and then it was her turn to chase us. We were not playing the game fairly, Girlie couldn't catch us. She came around the corner and our teacher, Mr Hugo Gottolile, was stooping down doing something to his motorbike. Girlie picked up a stick and hit him across the bottom, smack bang, he turned and gave her a cut with a stick then.

When I was going to school my teacher, Colin Thorn, understood stubborn children. There was a word in the old history book about King Alfred who burnt the cakes. I couldn't say this word. He said the word for me and and told me to repeat it after him. I kept repeating it to myself. He knew I could say it and he said, 'I can sit here as long as you, Ida', and then I knew he wasn't going to let me go until I did say it, even if it was after school. The rest of the children weren't allowed to go home until I said the word. My sisters and brother also were there so I had to get up then and say the word aloud.

Girlie and I, when we were young girls, would follow Mr Montgomery, the surveyor, around when he was surveying. He was a very nice man.

We used to go to school and play 'the charge of the light brigade'. The boys with sticks would stand at the bottom of the hill, us girls at the top with sticks, and we would charge at each other.

The girls made houses out of vines, we dressed up with vines around our necks, and what fun we used to have going fishing on the rocks. We were all done up.

When officials came across from Hobart, Sir James O'Grady, Police Commissioner Lord, and others, the Warden from the islands, Mr A.W. Burbury, a lawyer, and the councillors, came up to the school. We were the only dark children who were going there just at that time. They gave us the once over. We were told to straighten up our shoulders and look at them fair in the face. I don't think I've ever forgotten Commissioner Lord. I think I'd know him again if I ever saw him. I don't know what he was thinking, but I knew what I was thinking. We stood up and said, 'Yes, sir, No, sir'. We had a good teacher to tell us what to do.

We were always brought up by our mother and father to think of ourselves as good as the next one. We came into the world head first and we go out feet first, and that goes for everybody, without the breech baby. So Europeans are made no better, and they smell just the same when they pass away, so there is no difference. God made us all—as long as we get by and try to help people and not be so greedy by wanting everything. People who just have enough are as happy as the ones that have too much. I remember some people the more they got they more they wanted. That's why there are so many poor people today.

Some of the white people were reared by the Aboriginal people. A few families reared a lot up. They learnt to love them as they did their own.

IRISHMAN'S RIDE

We finally got push-bikes to get to school on—one to a family. One child would ride along the road, then walk on, leaving the bike for the next child who came along. It was called the Irishman's Ride.

There was a lot of skipping when I was going to school—skip all the way down the road, skip back—there to learn and listen. I can remember Mr Colin Thorn asking me what was that letter. I said it was a snake, although he wanted me to say 's'. I'd get up and say the wrong thing, then tell him I couldn't learn. Sometimes, though, I'd say something right. I liked writing. I always had problems putting the pen in the right hand, and when he wasn't looking I put the pen back in the left hand. When we got outside we would have tug-o'-wars, boys against girls, play hide-and-go-seek, and hares-and-hounds. We'd drop paper all down the beach then the others would have to follow the trail. And what a job they'd have. But we'd be back again. We were pretty bold, and then we'd hide up in the vines and they'd be singing out that the school was in, but we wouldn't answer. We could hear them but we wouldn't come down. That shows you just what we used to do. We were a wild mob.

After attending Lughrata for about five years we were burnt out at Howell's, as I describe later, and we went to Robertdale on Marshall Bay where Uncle Johnnie Smith and Gran' Aunt Millie lived. We were there when I left school at about fourteen years of age.

INTRODUCTIONS

My Great-Great-Grandfather, Andrew Armstrong, was born in 1814 and was married in St Joseph's Church, at 44 Margaret Street, Launceston, in 1842, the same year it was built. Now it's called the Church of the Apostles, Sacred Heart. My Great-Grandfather, Andrew Armstrong, was baptised at Stanley on 12 October 1847, the son of Andrew and Jane Armstrong, nee Foster. They were living at Arthur River, on the west coast with William Proctor and his family.

MARRIAGES

A few marriages occurred in 1830. A few have been so civilised as to contract marriages after the approved fashion of Europeans. The first took place at Launceston. Two who had long resided in the families of colonists were formally united in St John's Church, Launceston August 16th, 1830 (source unknown).

DUCK HOLES AND QUICKSAND

As a child I spent many a day playing on the beach at Robertdale which was called the 'duck hole'. My friend 'Ky' Sylvia Maynard, her sister Ena, and brother Oswald came with their mother, Maria, to see us. My mother and Maria told us we could go on the beach and walk in the water, but not to go too far out.

While on the beach we would eat currants that grew on the banks. We had no bathers, only bloomers or trousers with the legs cut off. We couldn't swim, but we tried to. All the girls went out further than we should have. The waves got bigger and bigger and lifted us off our feet. A great big fish like a stingray with big eyes on the top of its head chased us to the shore. We told Uncle Johnny Smith who looked it up in the fish book. It was called a Boat Ray, and could swing its tail around and cut our legs off. We never ever went out so far again. I feel that the good Lord sent that fish to warn us against going out so far.

It was after this adventure that we girls sat down on the beach to rest. Ena, the eldest, told us about the facts of life. The way Ena explained was simple and beautiful, and I shall always remember what she said—clean, nothing nasty, the simple facts of life.

Up the river at Marshall Beach is quicksand. Ky and I were playing up the river, when I felt my feet going down in the sand. I tried to get my feet out but they were going further and further down. Ky climbed a tree that was leaning over the quicksand, she gave me a stick to hold on to and pulled me out. I was in a terrible mess and frightened. I told Ky to be careful and not tread where I had been. Our parents had told us not to go too far up the river, and of course we shouldn't have been there.

EARTH TREMORS

Uncle Johnny Smith and Gran' Aunt Millie lost all their children, but they lived a long time—to a ripe old age. We had earth tremors when we lived at Robertdale. One was a nasty one, so Mum and another lady ran outside with us. All the crockery fell down.

When we looked over in the other paddock, Uncle Johnny and Gran Aunt were out at the wood heap. We went over and asked them why they were not frightened—we were only children. They said in their time they used to have earth tremors often, bad ones too. They had a lot of thunder storms, a lot of fork lightning. Uncle lived until he was eighty-four. Aunty was seventy-six. We were very young when he died, but we can still remember it all.

THE WHEATLEYS

There was a family of Wheatleys at Killiecrankie. They were fishermen. There was a story in the paper about them on 8 July 1945. The skipper, William Wheatley, was sighted and his blind son, Clifford, acted as crew. Wheatley sr was a fisherman all his life while his son, blinded as a young man, followed the calling by sense of touch, and 'sailed by the winds on his face'. They used to take it in turns to steer, the father at night, the son by day. The Wheatley descendants are still at Killiecrankie and scattered around Flinders Island.

Amy Wheatley

I knew Amy Wheatley when she came to Killiecrankie. I was eleven years old when she first came there in a fishing boat, and there she had to work. Cliff sharpened up the little axe for her and she chopped all the wood for Grandpa Wheatley. She knew how to chop wood, too! The hardest wood going, sheoak, she'd have to cut for her little stove. Then she went from Killiecrankie, where we all lived, where the boat was lying in the bay, to Lughrata with a horse and sled carrying a lot of fish to sell. It was about eleven miles. She needed to find someone to get them to sell at Whitemark. Another time Amy walked from Killiecrankie to Robertdale with a part of the motorboat engine. It was very heavy, but Amy did it. Then it had to go to Whitemark to Henry Briant to get fixed up.

She used to dig all the garden to grow the vegetables. Cliff Wheatley made a slip around the western side of Killiecrankie Bay around Hawks Nest way, then he made a ramp to pull the boat up on the rocks. Amy used to help bag up the crays and we also helped her. She could stand the cold, I don't know how she did it. The Wheatley family had a stone-age stove, and Amy baked good bread. Amy and Cliff got an old truck and equipment and then they used to take the crays down to the airport at Pats River and to bring home the groceries for everyone who didn't have a horse or cart. Once when I was with Amy the truck broke down in King Pine Gully, near Robertdale, and we had to drive all the way to Killiecrankie in reverse. Coming home we had groceries for Uncle Bun at the tin mine but we couldn't stop because if we did we couldn't get it started again. We had to throw the potatoes and the onions off. He wasn't pleased.

THE FIRE

When I was about eight or nine and living at Howell's a fire was lit and got out of control. Dad was away shearing. We four children were with Mum. Judy Beeton and her son, Rosland, were at the house with us. There was a lot of scrub around the house, which caught fire, too. The only things left in the end were a box of clothes, two jerry pots and the baker (camp oven), which was still useable. The damper inside was burnt to charcoal. We had to walk across the hot ashes in bare feet to get to the main road and to Brimworth where we waited for Dad. Dad had been away shearing at the Inner Sister Island and he turned up that same day. He wouldn't believe us when we said we were burnt out. Morton Maynard, a cousin who was a good carpenter, helped Dad to build a new place at Robertdale. All we had left after the fire were the clothes we stood up in. It was told to us after the fire that a white man had lit the fire knowing that it would burn us out. He said, 'I will fix those black bastards'.

THE BULL

When I was fourteen or fifteen I had to get the cows out of the garden, so I picked up a stick, it wasn't a very good one. I went down to the bottom paddock to get the cows and I saw them just the other side of the fence. The fence wasn't the best but it was good enough. I saw our neighbours bull, he wasn't so very old but he was quite old enough, and he was there with one of the cows which was called Snowy. I was always brought up to leave them and just bring the others, there was three more to bring and they were very tame—I thought I could get them away.

I climbed through the fence holding the stick. They all walked along the road and the bull came last. But he decided that he wasn't going to go and that was going to make short work of me. So, before I knew where I was, I was butted and my stick broke. He kept on butting me until I fell to the ground in the bracken ferns. The cows were that tame they just wouldn't go away, they stayed there too.

I had to act quickly, so I rolled on my side, my legs drawn up. Bracken ferns were sticking into them and I knew that bull was looking at me. I couldn't dare move or look. It was lucky I had a lot of clothes on. He knelt down but he knelt on the clothes and he even came around to smell my mouth to see whether I was still breathing, but I had my hand across my mouth and I wouldn't, couldn't breathe.

I prayed for the old cows to go away but they were there waiting for me to get up and bring them home. So I don't know just how long that bull was there, but I couldn't move and I couldn't look. Then I counted all the footsteps when the cows went away, I just don't know where they were going. Then I thought that the bull must have gone after Snowy. The fence wasn't so far away, in fact it was very close, and I thought, well then, it's now or never.

One side of my leg was numb, but I managed to drag it and get through the fence. I think the bull did come after me but I got up towards the hill as fast as I could go, and I was crying and screaming. My sister Esme was getting kindling and she was singing out, 'What's the matter?' I told her I was chased by the bull, so she ran to tell Dad. He thought that I was dead. His face was white as a sheet and he ran to get the gun, put the cartridge in it and down he came. He passed me on the way and I told him what the matter was. I said the bull will chase you too, and he did, but my father had the cartridges there and he put a couple a shots into him. The bull took off down to his own place as hard as ever he could go.

I was very frightened for months, I didn't go to a doctor, even now nobody can come up to me and pat me on the shoulder or anything. I still get a fright and at nights I'd scream out. I wasn't so far away from the road and I could hear a man going home on his motorbike when all this was happening. But I couldn't even get up and scream. They got someone to shoot it the next morning, he was just a nasty little bull.

SNAKES

When we were girls we used to watch snakes and the blue-tongue goannas having fights. The snakes would bite the blue-tongues, who would put up a good fight. The blue-tongue would crawl to a bunch of buzzies (bidgee-widgees or burrs), looking very sick, he would try to get under as far as he could. Each day we would go to see the goanna. It would be there for a long time, but something they used to eat saved them. Perhaps it may have been the buzzies, I don't know, but they didn't die.

When I was going to school there were snakes everywhere. My brother, my sisters and I saw a log on the road on a culvert, there we saw all these baby snakes, there were more than a dozen. I don't know if there were two families, we didn't stay very long because we were not sure where the mother or father snakes were—they wouldn't be far away. Snakes have big families. The Marshall (the road from Emita to Robertdale) was a place for lots of snakes. Another time a female snake took to us. We found a big stone and hit her with it. It was just as well we did, but it was a cruel way to do it. We jabbed her stomach and all the baby snakes came out—some of the stuff got on my arm. We got home as fast as we could and I washed my arm straight away. Dad told us we were never to be cruel. We, like all the children, had to carry a stick.

Dad used to go looking for water with a forked stick and when he found water he dug a well. We would go with him and the next morning often there would be a big water snake in the well, the red-bellied black snake. There were a lot of snakes on Flinders Island when I was a girl and where we lived at Killiecrankie there was a lot of scrub. There was a lagoon I had to go through, it was the only water at the place—our cows used to go through it in the thickest part and there were snakes all over the place. If we took the short cut through Pinescrub across the hills, we had to watch out for the tiger snakes. The tiger snake has a head shaped like a diamond. They would get in the toilets up the back yard. A toilet was a large hole dug in the ground with a little house built over the top. It was hard to make it snake-proof. To keep the toilet clean we put ashes and Phenyle in it. If a snake got down the hole we put the suplhur down to get them out. We had the copper head snakes which would come to the house or sheds looking for mice or rats. They were thin, long snakes and very cheeky. We had to put milk out, and be very quiet so they would come out to drink the milk and we would be ready with a stick to kill them. We had the whip snake and the grass snake. I was listening to Harry Butler talking about goannas, he said people think they are death adders. I was getting the cows in one afternoon, I was going with my stick when I saw what I thought was a goanna, I got a little closer to it but that was no goanna. I watched it crawl away, it was just like a death adder, the marks on it, thick body, and the thin rat-like tail. I went home and looked it up in a snake book. I told Dad I wasn't going along that track again. We got a dog to rouse the cows out. Dad reckoned there wasn't a death adder. He had never seen one, but I believe what I saw.

The women and the men all worked on Chappell Island amongst the tiger snakes and the 'Barking Brilla'. (The 'Barking Brilla' is the name for the snake-infested saltbush (barilla) on Chappell Island—the snakes make a warning noise when you get too close). There were a lot of snakes there. The famous snake expert, Eric Worrell, told me they were the second most deadly snakes in Australia. The heads of this tiger snake on Chappell seemed to be bigger than those of the snakes on Flinders.

WORK AND PLAY

Then we used to go working, ploughing, over in the fifteen acres at Killiecrankie. We'd do the ploughing with a old plough, then we helped my brother Owen to mark the lambs and dip them. Later we'd probably try to get a kangaroo with old Les, the dog. He'd go away and catch the kangaroo and then he'd come back to us. We'd look in his mouth to see whether he had any blood or fur, then we'd tie something around his neck and tell him to show us where the roo was. Probably he would have two or three lined up for us to carry back.

We would go over to Palana for a drive on the Sunday, see Mrs Eden, Mary and Annie Eden, Mr Jack Eden and Mr George Boyes. They'd always make us welcome as Dad used to work there for them.

We used to go to the Nor'East River, just spearing flounders, and sometimes snaring, and when we were camping over there Annie and Mary Eden used to come over to see us at the river. There would be a lot of badgers [wombats] and they were great big ones. When they were caught in a snare they'd uproot everything. Dad used to kill them to make rugs, and I used to hide and cover my face so I couldn't see it. We caught one at the Nor'East River once and when I went back recently I said I could remember where the lupins were. They were still there, beautiful blue lupins. The snare was further up the hill and that was where we caught this big badger.

We'd go fencing with an axe, and have to clean the line of fence right down both sides, by the time we got home it would be late.

We'd have a lot of books and papers given to us. Mrs Eden's girls used to give us the *Post* and the *Pix*, *Weekly Times*, *Women's Weekly*. They used the *Australasian*. We had photos of all the cricketers. We were pretty good with the scissors, cutting up all this paper. We would paste them on the wall so we could look at them but we'd put the mess down behind the bed before Mum found it all. She wanted us to do our cutting up then take our mess out.

Esme, my sister, liked to cook. She'd always be combing her hair, looking in the mirror, making herself look nice, but not me—I'd be down, with dungaree trousers on, helping Dad outside, growing the vegetables. Often Girlie would be with me as we didn't like being inside. It came pretty hard for us when we married and had to cook. But we were growing our garden, growing our tomatoes, potatoes, turnips, and onions.

We had to carry water to do our washing. It was nothing to see a couple of snakes in the well. We'd pull up the bucket, carry the water home, make lye water with ashes, and bleach our clothes. The children had to help also.

Ruby and I went for fire-wood. We took the horse and sledge, and ran into a stump. The sledge went sideways. When we arrived home we took the wood off and let the horse go. Johnnie Maynard found the sledge crooked and called us up to ask us what we did to it. We said we didn't do anything. He knew we did. We told a wicked lie. He said, 'When you grow up, young women, remember always to say "no"'. I said to Ruby when Johnnie went away, 'What was that all about?' But Ruby said she didn't know. We didn't know much about the facts of life. When we became young women and went to a dance at Pinescrub, I said to Ruby, 'Do you know what your father was talking about now?' Ruby said, 'Yes we know now'.

Dad gave myself and my cousin, Dulcie Beeton, a job for two days threshing trefoil grass to get seed. At the end of the two days we had twelve chaff bags full. I accidently cracked Dulcie over the head with my pitchfork, so Mum came down. She reckoned we were too dangerous, and told us to leave off. We received three pounds each.

We used to cut bracken ferns with the fern-hook, or use a slasher to cut the tea-tree and other small trees. Together we would move logs with a crowbar onto a stump then burn them. It looks lovely of a night. We used to like doing it until we moved a log with the crowbar and saw a snake under it.

My first job was kangarooing: snaring and skinning them, then pegging them out on a tree to dry. I would then bundle them and send them to Melbourne in the trading boat to Younghusband and Company, skin merchants.

I received seven pounds, my first pay. My sister Girlie helped me. I never went out to work, I kept a vegetable garden. Girlie and Esme went out to do domestic work, but I didn't want to.

GHOSTS

There are all the old ghost stories. You start telling the ghost stories and you'd be all sitting around in the room and, when you were just about finished, everyone would be sitting around the fire, all the chairs close together. So we'd wait to go to bed at the same time as everyone else.

There were a lot of ghost stories around. There was the story of the ghost on Tin Kettle Island, Uncle Johnny Smith's story. When he was a child they were left alone in the shed on Tin Kettle one night—his parents might have gone across to Woody Island. They heard the dog barking. They pulled aside the curtain and there was an old black woman with a basket in her hand, bobbing up and down. They all got into bed together and never got out to look, of course.

I think that years ago they did see things—justice had to be done. They say there was a murder on Tin Kettle in the early days.

Tanner's Bay is a shocking place for ghosts. I don't know what happened there. There's an atmosphere about the place. Stanley Blythe agreed with me. At certain times of the month, when the tide comes right up, there is a noise underneath like a horse galloping. It's not a good place.

At Guncarriage pictures used to fall off the wall.

At Lady Barron, where the motel is now, there's a short cut down to Yellow Beach. There was a murder there, and a figure of a man in a white shirt has been seen.

At Bull Head scrub on Babel Island, from the Gulch to the West Beach, you could hear a woman screaming. But it was really a tree branch rubbing against another tree. My father found this out. The Armstrongs were never frightened, they'd go and have a look.

ANIMALS

Mum would let us go over to see Charlie Jones. His cat had a lot of kittens up at Pinescrub, and he called them kitty one, kitty two, kitty three, up to kitty six. Then he made up a song. He had a small block of land and he would get grass from everywhere. His horses and cows were always fat. He'd get the hoe and dig a hole and put the grass and seed in, all kinds of clover, kikuyu grass and even buffalo, I think he had there.

Dad brought a wild baby pig home. We reared him and called him Darby. When he grew up he was very tame, a lovely pet. We had to walk three miles (nearly five kilometres) to get the mail, and we would take Darby with us. When they killed him for Christmas we children cried. We couldn't eat Darby.

In Dad's time there used to be plenty of goats on the old house flat and they often climb the mountain to feed.

Girlie, when a small child, had a pet petrel. It was a very small bird which we found on one of the Pascoe Islands. The petrel is different from the mutton-bird.

One day Mum was bathing my baby sister, Ila, when Vern Green arrived. Vern Green had all boys in his family. He looked at Ila and said, 'Oh, she's only a little girlie'. Ila has been Girlie ever since.

MADAM

There was a lady everyone called 'Madam' because she was loved and highly respected. She treated everyone the same. One day I met Madame Virieux on the road to Whitemark. I had never seen her in my life before. She talked to me about Mum and Dad for a while. A motor car came along and we got dust all over ourselves, so she told me when they were all young people the Aboriginal descendants used to take their small boats to town [Launceston] to get food. The Europeans used to grow the gardens, and they used to help one another. She was a very nice lady, what she meant was people had more time in the earlier days to stop and talk, but with the cars there just didn't seem the time.

HORSES AND COWS

Old Peter was a stallion. There was Fanny and Flirt, and Dad had a mare called Kit.

One day I rode Flirt to Palana to see the two Miss Edens. I was running late, it was dark and I knew Mum and Dad would be worried. So I took a short cut home even though I wasn't a very good rider. When we came to a dry creek, which Flirt was used to jumping, I couldn't get her to go over. I had to go around the road and that took me much longer. Dad met me and I told him what Flirt had done. He said, 'That was funny, she always jumps. What would you have done if she had jumped?' I said, 'Hung on to the saddle' and Dad replied 'When you landed on the other side you would have been on the ground or your neck broken'. Flirt wouldn't jump because she knew I couldn't ride properly, and she knew I had never been on a horse that had jumped before.

One time Auntie Belle and I had to get the calves in. One calf was big and we had a chain on it although I don't know what was wrong with her. We grabbed the chain and the calf took off. The faster the calf went the faster we went. We didn't let the chain go—over the tussocks we went. We fell over so we had to let go and we started laughing. Then we had to get my sisters to come with us to get the calf in.

Dad had some cows we used to get from Mr Keith Blyth. We would break and tame the young calf heifers. When the calves grew up Keith took the heifers in. Frank said they will go in the bail themselves. Keith went down to look and the heifers were so quiet that when they went in the bail each one put its foot out for the leg rope. Keith gave Girlie and I the cows to milk, and we would train the young calves. We had a cow named Granny Allport. Dad brought her from Dr Allport and Mum growled at him for getting one so old. But she couldn't have been too old, because she had a beautiful heifer which we called Lipstick. One old cow got into my vegetable garden and I got stuck into her with a dropper. Another time I ran to get the dropper, I trod on one and the other end came up and hit me on the forehead. That was when I first learnt to swear.

We would go walking in the bush and cut the grass trees [Xanthorrea]. We would take a little tomahawk to cut the roots or shoots of the grass trees then eat the bread inside. We ate the stems of the bull rushes.

My father had to take a bull to Palana. Mum said that he should get a couple of heifers or a cow or something to take with the bull, but he tried to take the bull alone. Dad was on Kit, she was a lovely mare. It was just as well he was though because, halfway to the Quoin, the bull decided he was coming back and he went to charge Kit. But Kit was too swift for the bull. She had to jump. She jumped the bull, right over the top. Dad had to hang on but that taught him a lesson. He had to let the bull go and that was the end of it. Mum had the pleasure to tell him that he should have taken notice of her in the first place.

My father used to do contract work, mainly fencing, and he

would take my brother Owen and also young boys and men from Cape Barren Island. Dad also sheared sheep. I would go snaring with him and Owen and my sister Girlie would come too, we would go fencing and putting up the droppers at the North East River. Dad would also go with Mr Montgomery, the surveyor, and help him at different times. Dad had a horse he called Currymore, and one called Lady which he got off Tom Gunter. Dad had a razor strap which he used to give us a couple of cuts across the legs or on the hands. He never used it much, he would talk to us and there was a lot of authority in his voice. He always banged his fist down on the table but I was very stubborn, just like a mule. I was sent to my room once and when it was time for tea I wouldn't go down. Dad or Mum would come to get me and that would make my sisters laugh, and Owen my brother as well. They would call me the mule, which would make me worse, although they were very careful not to let Dad or Mum hear them.

While he was working at the north end of Flinders Island, Dad, if it was early, would go up and play cards and crib after work with Mr Frank Boyes, who was from Hobart. He would play to the early hours of the morning, and then take old Fanny or Flirt home with the buggy.

My father used to keep the water boiling for the Emita sports. Mr Phillgate was the teacher at Lady Barron school. He went to get some hot water from Dad and told him that they had brought a very sick man down from Cape Barren Island. Dad asked him if was he a dark man or white man. Mr Phillgate knew the answer but he also knew his manners. He said that he would go and find out. Gerald Phillgate came back and said that it was Mr Hubert Maynard. Dad said if there was a hole in the ground he would have gone through it because Mr Hubert Maynard was very dark. Gerald put Dad in his place by not saying whether he was black or white.

Everyone was born with a handle to their name.

SHEEP DOGS

Dad was working shearing on the Inner Sisters when George Blyth's dog gave birth to pups. George picked one out for himself, one for his brother and the smallest and ugliest he gave to Dad. We called him Les; Keith's dog was Bill. We trained Les for kangaroos and wallabies and oppossums. Bill's and George's dogs were trained for sheep.

Bill would bring sheep from Palana to Robertdale by himself, Keith would go home, open the gates and have his tea while Bill brought the sheep down. One time Bill was overdue. Keith was worried and went to look for him and the sheep. When Keith found them, Bill was sitting by a new born lamb which he couldn't make walk. So he was waiting for Keith to come back for him.

Most dogs in those days when they met on the roadsides or wherever would start fighting, but these three would never fight. They seemed to know that they were brothers and just lay down together.

To think back to those good times on Flinders Island with Dad is wonderful.

SPORTS AND DANCES

Granny Beckie was going to the Emita sports and was dressed in her best with pale-pink silk stockings.

While we all waited for Mr Woods to pick us up, my Grandfather's dog came up to Gran and pee'd on her new stockings. Granny Beckie told off Grandfather and then she took her stockings off and went to the creek to wash them. It was a hot morning so the stockings dried out before Mr Woods came.

In the book *Mission to the Islands* my gran'father Harry Armstrong is mentioned. He used to take them about in his boat called the *Julia*.

A lot of my people used to chew charcoal. We used it for toothpaste.

We had to fight our own battles. We got a hammering if we came home and said someone called us black. We stuck up for ourselves and weren't allowed to come home to tell tales. We had to get back in and fight. I mean, that was all right. There were only a few white children going to school and we had good teachers who saw that there was fair play. There was a white boy, we used to call him 'father', he used to see that there was fair play. It was never two onto one, it didn't matter who was having a fight. He was one of the best at school.

You had to be white. At the dances you had to put on all the powder and the Pond's cream, and black tulip powder. The men used to put hair oil on their hair. We still do it now, getting the powder the colour of your skin. If you were one shade you had to put another shade on top of it. You could see the funny side of it. But then if we went to the dances it would hurt. There wasn't many of our own people there to dance with and often we had to sit down all night. Strangers from the mainland would probably know who we were, but they wouldn't be half as bad as those from Flinders Island who thought themselves somebody important when they were in the dance hall.

When we joined in the square dance we all got up to dance, but the white dancers all fell out. That shows you how ignorant they were. Mr Wheatley came with us the first time and, when he got home, he said they were as ignorant as the pigs from Schouten Hill. I had never heard that saying before.

Mr Dickie Smith used to go dancing in his bowyangs. He took Annie Eden for a dance on Flinders Island, and as they were starting the square dancing a girl got her hair caught in a nail. She couldn't go on as they had to get her hair from the nail. They used to have all classes of people—it was funny when you went to the dances—silver-tails, golden-tails, copper-tails, the half-castes sitting around the door, a policeman (a senior constable) standing outside the door. Those were our dances.

Sometimes I can remember my mother used to go to church at Emita Hall. It was the same at church, they just wouldn't speak to us. If they did, they were frightened to open their mouths too wide unless someone might hear them. That was the last straw. But when you saw these people in their own homes, or you met them by themselves, you couldn't wish for better people. It was only when they had a gathering of their own people and you mixed with them. One of our girls found a letter that one of the teachers had written to one of the white ladies. It said that some of the half-castes were coming to a dance at the same school. But later on the same white woman used to get us ready for the big concerts at Whitemark, my word, she'd make a good job of us too.

We used to go to dances at Pine Scrub, across the hills from Robertdale and Killiecrankie. We would walk, taking the short cuts. We would have to stay all night and have saddles as pillows.

Most of the dances were at Robertdale, after shearing, mutton-birding, Christmas and Easter. All my relations and friends would come over from Cape Barren.

The band at the dances was usually Grandfather Neuto Everett who could play the accordian and violin, Uncle Albert Everett on the mouth organ and Uncle Clem Beeton on the accordian and violin. At one time when a lot of the men were working on the mines between Robertdale and Killiecrankie, Joe Shegog and Elvie came to play the accordian. Joe was a very good singer. Their son Kevin and Ronnie are also good singers and Bill Wheatley played the accordian at these dances.

When we were children we were not allowed outside, we all had to learn how to dance. The parents were very strict about not letting the children outside.

When Kentdale was turned into a stud farm the trainers and the jockeys of the horses used to come up to Robertdale to the dances.

We used to go to a lot of dances at Lady Barron. They were good dances too. Auntie Lucy Thomas was one of the best singers and she also sang in church with the Robertson brothers.

We had a dance at Robertdale at our house. Dad was working away for the day but knew the dance was being held at home. We had a spring cleaning and we took all the crockery in the bread dish outside to be washed ready for the night's supper. We forgot to bring the bread dish back in, and we were all dancing and enjoying ourselves. Dad came home with old Fanny in the cart in the dark. The cart wheel caught the dish with the crockery in it and there was broken crockery everywhere. Mum had to calm Dad down and then everyone decided to throw in some money to get some crockery whenever we could get down to the store.

Mum would have mutton birds and damper cooked for the dancers who had travelled a long way to our house. Morton Green and his family would travel from Lady Barron to Killiecrankie.

We were brought up to get up with whoever asked us to dance, except if they were drunk.

BLACK TRACKING

We did our share of black tracking. If we were out in the bush, we would make signs to get home. We could track down snakes. We could tell which way the snakes were going on the soft sand.

We learned to tell if the snake was going away or towards the house. A snake never liked to travel over buffalo grass—they would go over it slowly, as they couldn't cling to the leaves.

FIRE PLACES

Most of the houses including my home had big fire places, made out of stones and clay. You could put logs on as big as a fence post. We used to whitewash our fireplaces—they still do on Cape Barren Island, with clay. At Pinescrub the clay from the beach was beautiful, a blue cast right through it.

MUSIC

My brother Owen had a Columbia gramophone, we would dance and sing at home. We had lovely dances, people would come and Owen would play records for us.

RECEIPTS

Everyone used to keep their receipts on a piece of wire hanging on the wall. Even when they became yellow with age they would take them down to the shed and hang them up. Everyone was frightened to throw away a receipt because if you couldn't find the receipt you would have to pay for an item again.

Sometimes if the receipt didn't have a duty stamp on it you would have to pay over again.

BUSHRANGERS
(as told to me by Uncle Johnny Smith Jnr)

There were sealers at the Hogan group of islands with some other men and they were getting seals when they looked up and saw a boat. They knew what bushrangers were, so Uncle Johnny and crew jumped in their boat and cleared off for Flinders as fast as they could. There was another time when they were caught. They had a kerosene tin of dough-boys cooking when three bushrangers came. The bushrangers were hungry, they didn't have any food, so they asked what Uncle Johnny and his crew were cooking. They said 'Dough-boys'. The bushrangers made my people eat some, and even though they said that you could eat dough-boys at any time, the bushrangers waited for a while to see if anything happened. They thought the dough-boys might be poisoned. The man who ate two dough-boys said, 'Shoot me, you cowardly bugger. I can't eat anymore'. They seemed to like Martin Cash. I don't think they could trust Brady and there was another man, called Morgan, they didn't trust.

Chapter two
The middle years

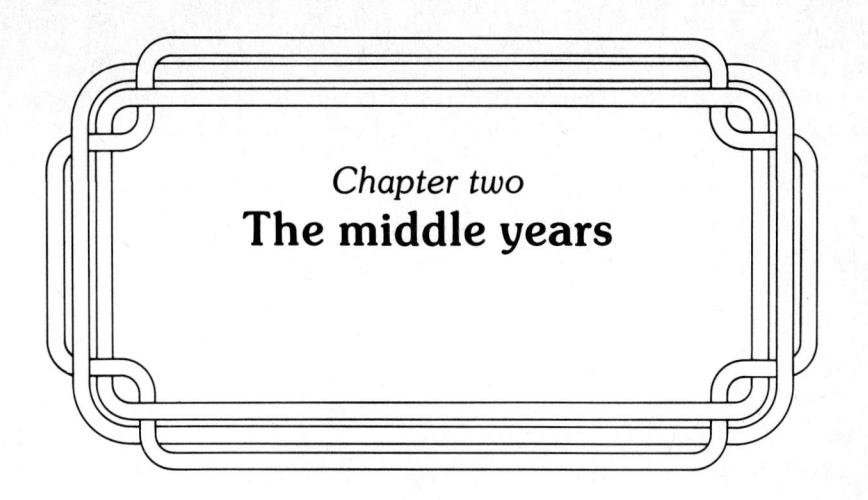

MARRIAGE AND CHILDREN

I was married on 30 September 1939, at Killiecrankie, Flinders Island, under the gum trees. I was twenty years old and married Marcus Sydney West. Emily Killworth and Andrew Reynolds were witnesses, Girlie was matron of honour, and her husband Tim was our best man. The Reverend Charles Brammall of the Church of England married us. We went on our honeymoon at the Quoin, just a few miles from Killiecrankie, milking cows for Mr Keith Blyth. I am sure we shifted around more than any other couple on Flinders Island.

    I had a daughter, Lenna, born at the Queen Victoria Hospital in Launceston on 27 July 1940, and a son born on 25 April 1945, VE Day, also at the Queen Victoria Hospital. We called him Darrell Arthur. I wasn't allowed to eat meat for a few days after Darrel was born, but when I could the sister said we were having only vegetables for the day, because the butchers and everyone else were out celebrating, and doing the black-out stroll. Everyone from the hospital was out celebrating also.

    My husband used to work at fishing, dairying, mutton-birding, harvesting and working for the council on the roads. I lived in tents over at Tanners Bay, on the west coast of Flinders Island. I was

My daughter Lenna.

left there with the children and we didn't even have doors to shut. The roos jumped around the tent all night on the hollow ground. I was left by myself when the men went to West End to bag up the crays. I had my happy moments in my marriage. My husband had a drink problem and I was as stubborn as a mule, but we were married for seventeen years.

Before we moved to Hobart Markie worked hard. We earned a lot of money but it was never put to good use. I think that was the reason I eventually got divorced in 1960 in Hobart. I didn't like to see good money going down the drain. I tried to rear my children the best I could with the help of a good lawyer, the Police Boys Club and the Reverend Charles Brammall. I had to go to work. I wasn't used to electricity and when I first had to use a polisher I had to get someone to help me to keep it from running away. In the end I got used to it.

Markie and I lived at Mr Peter Grant Hays' place at the Quoin. A fire started at Palana and all the men had to go there to help. There were fires all up the coast of Flinders so they left me to watch the Quoin. I went and found all the sack bags I could and went down and put them in the water trough. We kept an eye on the Quoin. I looked up over to Mr Keith Blyth's paddock which is called Baxters, and sparks had got into the grass. Darrell and I went across to the fire with our bags and bushes. I didn't have a phone to ring anywhere. We started to work. There was a drain and windmill close by. I wasn't feeling too good but I had to stick to it. Darrell helped with a bush. The men at Palana saw the fire at the Quoin, so they sent Mr Athol Blyth to help me. I was glad to see him and we got to work hosing and using buckets of water from the windmill. Darrell saw Mr Athol Blyth putting water in the drain to stop the fire crossing, so he thought that he would make water to help. I had to tell him he was a rude little boy and to turn his back. Mr Athol Blyth was saying, 'Good little boy, we want all the water we can get'. Anyway the wind dropped, so we saved the paddock, and the men had put out the fire at Palana.

My daughter, Lenna, was brought up the same way that I was. She never had much of an education. She didn't start school until she was nine, and she left again when she was fourteen, and moved to Hobart to live with her Auntie.

The only things she knew how to do well were snaring, hunting, fishing and mutton-birding. She worked as a domestic in hospitals until she married.

Lenna came back to Killiecrankie from Hobart after about five years for a visit, and she saw a big change on the island. Most of the land our people owned was sold, and they had moved to the mainland (Tasmania and Victoria). Even her grandfather's farm at Killiecrankie had gone. She would have liked to see the island stay as it was. Now our people are scattered all over Tasmania.

One of her biggest dreams was to go to Arnhem Land. She applied for a study grant to go with Dr Rhys Jones and Dr Betty Meehan on a working trip, and she was up there for ten days living and working with the tribal Aboriginals. They accepted a Tasmanian Aborigine but they couldn't understand why her skin wasn't as dark as theirs. Every day they would look at her skin and they could see her skin get darker and they would smile at her.

Lenna couldn't talk to them, she had to make signs with her hands. She said many of the things that they did were not new to her. She can remember our own people teaching her such things as what shellfish to eat and how to cook them, going to the water hole to wash, what grass to use on the floors to lay on, hunting and snaring, burning off the land for new growth, for wild animals and to make hunting easier, and having the meals before dark so you could sit around the camp fire, talk, dance and sing. It took her back to her childhood.

Lenna said the time she spent there was one of the greatest in her life because it made her realise just how much an Aborigine she, and many more Tasmanians like herself, were. It was a warm feeling to know what you were—not just a half-caste from Flinders Island and Cape Barren.

FOOTBALL AND OTHER GAMES

On Flinders Island there used to be two football teams, Bass and Flinders, picked out from the children. One team was picked by Mrs Ray and the other by her husband, a school teacher at Whitemark. They were both Catholics, but Mr Ray got the Anglican kids who were the best footballers. Mr and Mrs Ray and Mrs Hammond were good to my children, teaching my daughter to wait on tables. They were probably a bit strict but it didn't hurt Lenna because when she had to go to work it all came naturally to her.

Lenna played basketball and netball, liked dancing, and both she and Darrell liked to twist around. I always loved the ballroom dancing and square dancing.

Lenna was a good runner, Darrell could run a three-legged race and the set race. Both of them were good at set races, because I taught them how to put their feet in a bag and run. It was the only thing I could win when I was going to school but I taught myself by practising every day. Lenna never took up any sport later on. She had to work, riding motor bikes and learning to drive cars. She got married and never had it easy but later she started working for the Aboriginal people and she liked it very much.

We joined the football club, but we often used to be called names. That didn't worry Darrell much because I told him that such things wouldn't hurt him. When they throw stones or something then its time for you to sing out. He was always a good sports boy, playing his sport.

Darrell played football at Perth in Tasmania, when we lived there. Once he was going for the ball and two opposing footballers were going through and they meant business. My son had to let the ball go and let fly with his fist. God gave him a pair of hands and he let fly. One player was put in the hospital. Just as well there were two big policemen standing by the fence. They said he had to do it in self-defence, because if he didn't get them they were going to get him—that's football.

They grow up into men, but I enjoyed football more when they were children. They didn't care if they won the game or not, as long as they were able to jump up, and play a game.

We went to a carnival once in Launceston, the players were all from other States. It was a proud moment for me with all those different Aboriginal people—I thought just how marvellously these Aboriginal people could play football. They used to run fast and they never tried to hurt anyone, they'd jump over the top of someone or try to get around them somehow. They never hurt anyone unless it was an accident. I was very proud of all my people from all States and when I went to Adelaide to a carnival there, twelve months or two years later, they seemed to be playing more like white people—if you can't win by fair means then win by foul, push and shove. A couple of women umpires were telling

My son Darrell, aged 17.

me that the men umpires had talked it over and had said that the white footballers should play how the Aboriginals play, 'cause they never try to hurt anyone.

I must have taken after my father, he could never fight with his hands but he would always speak out with his tongue.

Darrell used to play football on Flinders Island. He went to Albuera Street School in Hobart and he played football there too, but he never had any football boots. Then he used to go to the Hobart Police Boys' Club. They took him out and he played with the under-fifteens for the Tigers. They found guernseys and socks and boots, so he played with them for a long time. Then the school found out about it and he had to play with the schools. Tim, my brother-in-law, helped me buy another pair of football boots for him because he had a fairly big foot and took a man's size. I had no other money, only what I earned by myself.

One year they had to play Taroona High for the championship and Albuera won—my son kicked *so* many goals. I had a handkerchief to my eyes because all the Taroona High children were singing out and calling out his name, calling him 'black'. The more they called him 'black' the more he'd kick goals for his school. As he grew up he played with the Tigers (under nineteens) then for Perth, and later for North Launceston. That's where most of the Aboriginal boys played in Launceston. His grandfather was a member of the North Launceston Football Club, so Bobby Withers took him under his wing. I only wish that he had stayed there with North, many a game I went to see him play.

I had to be father and mother and go to meetings when there was only supposed to be men there. Darrell would always say, 'You had better go to the meeting, Mum. Some of the men would bring their wives and so I got that way that I went to every football match. I came down to work in Hobart, and Darrell joined up with Glenorchy and he played there for a long time. He played as full-forward and he would come home and talk football. After a while he got a job as coach, way up at Irish Town on the North West Coast. The year before he went they lost the grand final by one point, so Darrell went there just at the right time because of what he knew. They took out the grand final and even won a night game at Devonport (or somewhere). At one time they went to play

My son Darrell with Sir Douglas Nicholls.

the union. I was very proud of him. I could probably talk football all night and all day.

One day Darrell took me to the under fifteens, to the under nineteens, then to the reserves and then to the seniors. When I came home I could see football guernseys all night.

Darrell always did love a ball to play with. He'd juggle a stone or a tin all the way to school. I wasn't very rich when he was growing up, when he was four or five years old he wanted a ball, so we got rubber balls, tennis balls, then we ended up getting a football—so many footballs I got him in the end. He was picked for the Northern Tasmanian team and, although they didn't win, they asked him what good he did. He said that he shook hands to the Governor, so I suppose that was something. He was always a good footballer but he was probably too good in that he always tried to help his mates. That's how we lost to Glenorchy in a grand final one year. If he'd have kicked the ball he could have got a point, and that would have been enough to either win or draw the game. But he tried to pass it to someone, and then the other side got it, and that was the end of it. We always talk about it, even today.

DANCE AT CAPE BARREN

I went over to the hall at Cape Barren for the New Year's Eve ball. It was perhaps at the beginning of 1941, about a year after Major Davies, the politician, opened the hall. What a lovely dance it was, everyone had their Sunday best on. Ladies all in evening dresses, gentlemen in suits and ties. The Brown brothers had their band and, my word, they could play. Ben and Donald Brown and the younger Browns were there too. I had a blue dress and Girlie had a floral dress from Hordens Brothers in Sydney. A lot of dresses came from Winns in Sydney, Sydney Wake's in Melbourne and Sullivan's in Tasmania. We'd get them COD and pay at the Post Office. Ruby Maynard had a red velvet dress, Eileen Maynard and sister Molly looked very nice. Irene Priscilla was in red and looked lovely, also Mavis Summers looked very nice. But the one who was belle of the ball was Jessie Mansell, she was in all white. Una and Stella Mansell looked nice but Jessie took the cake, she was like an angel. I can still remember when she walked in the hall.

How we all looked at her, what a lovely dress. Bernard Maynard was my partner for the square dance. The late Hubert Maynard was a very good dancer.

There was a policeman on Flinders Island, George Hanlon, who was so well-liked and respected that when the people of Cape Barren heard he was leaving they held a dance at Cape Barren in his honour. The policeman and his wife started the dance by circling the floor. My father was later told by the policeman that both he and his wife felt like a king and queen.

Dances used to be held on the mutton-bird islands. We would dance on the grass floors of the birding sheds.

LETTER FROM GIRLIE TO IDA

Do you remember, Ida, the year of the long frocks? It was the year before Tim and I were married. You, Markie, Tim and myself went up to Cape Barren Island for Christmas. The year was, I think, 1939. We stayed at Auntie Mary's and Andrew Maynard's place. I was about as fat as a match. But looking back, I think it was the nicest Christmas I had, because I suppose it was the first one I had spent away from home. Do you remember their sports day? We walked up to the sports ground. It was a little different from our Emita sports on New Years day. When they had the Cup race, some of the Cape Barren boys climbed up a sheoak tree and gave a description of the horses and riders as they came past the winning post, and Andrew's horse had won the Cup. So, when we arrived back to Auntie Mary's after the sports she was very pleased, but said someone should have gone back to tell her earlier that Andrew's horse had won instead of keeping her waiting. Remember how we all said Grace before we had the meal and also the day we left Cape Barren for Lady Barron and home again? We came home with Tim in the 'Kerrinda'. Also on board with us was Uncle Bun Beeton and Renee Priscilla Thomas. Coming down through the passage a strong easterly wind came up and Renee got frightened and wanted to be put aboard the 'Renee', the Cape Barren sailing boat. She kicked up so much that we did put her on board and so we got to Lady Barron safely and before the 'Renee' did.

BROTHER-IN-LAW AND BILLY SAMUEL

My brother-in-law, Andy, was bringing a heifer over from Pinescrub one day. He was riding a horse and he took a short cut from Tanners Bay to Killiecrankie. He was going around the bushes, but the heifer was going through the bushes. Andy was going to give it up when he saw another man on a horse. The horse belonged to Charlie Jones and was being ridden bareback by Billy Samuel. The horse was called Tunny. Mr Billy Samuel, an Aborigine from Queensland, was a boxer. The heifer was going through the bushes, so Billy Samuel went through the bushes too. Billy Samuel was an expert in the bush, and they got the heifer to Killiecrankie.

Billy Samuel used to be at the Quoin with us doing some work. He would put on a clean shirt each evening and go over to another man and his wife and little girl to listen to the boxing on the wireless. The champion Mr Samuel would bob his head and put his fist out during the fighting. The little girl was looking at him and she said to him, 'Why don't you go home and wash your hands and face?' He told me, 'That's the best line ever put over me'. He said he had been called 'old smoke' or a 'big thunder cloud', but he reckoned that was the best. The little girl's father was going to hit her and Billy told him, 'You have never explained to her about coloured people'. So he did that and they were friends then, Mr Samuel and the little girl.

Mr Samuel told me that up in Queensland they saw white people rounding their cows and calves, and branding them. The Aboriginal people saw this, and the Aboriginal children had the branding irons in a fire ready to start branding their little brothers and sisters. I think that they did do one! There's a lot that should have been learnt years ago.

He also told me about his Uncle, Gerry Jerome, when he won his first fight, they asked him what he wanted in money. Instead of saying so much money, he said he wanted a new horse, saddle and bridle. That was what he wanted.

ABORIGINES SWIMMING

I was on Killiecrankie Beach with Auntie Sarah Beeton and her children and Billy Samuel was on the beach somewhere as well. Billy, a full-blood Aborigine, was staying with us and he was a champion boxer in his day. Dad liked him very much. I was sitting with Aunt Sarah when I looked towards the bay and saw three small boys, they seemed to be sitting on the water, but they were moving. I said to Aunt Sarah, 'Look at your boys'. The reason they looked like they were sitting on the water was because they were sitting on Billy's back. Billy was like a whale. He put his head up, blew out his nose and would then go under a little way. The boys were having a wonderful time. Billy was a very good swimmer, he and his brothers had taught themselves to swim, he said.

FLOODS AT KILLIECRANKIE

Girlie and Tim lived in a hut near a swamp and we lived in a tent not far away. Auntie Sarah Beeton, Elvin and Les had a tent in the scrub towards the beach at Killiecrankie. We were all snaring for kangaroo and wallaby. Wallaby snares were called footies because we caught them by the foot, and the ones for roos were neckies as they were caught by the neck. The rain came—it rained and rained and the swamp filled up. Markie and I were in bed. We were roused up because the tent was leaking and water was coming in underneath. We got up, dressed, put knee boots on and went over to Girlie and Tim's hut thinking that they would be dry. When we were nearly there Markie said, 'The water is nearly up to the hut'. We had a lantern and we knocked at the door noticing the water coming through the door, Girlie said, 'Come in'. We told her that we were flooded out and that the water was coming through their door. Tim and Girlie had been in bed asleep. We lit the lamp and they couldn't believe that the water was coming through the door. They opened their eyes when the two, unused, jerry pots came floating out from under the bed and across the floor. They got dressed and then we talked it over, we had to go over to Auntie Sarah and the boys' tent. We started through the bush to Auntie Sarah when we heard someone cooee-ing. It was raining very hard. We listened. It was coming from up the track, cooee, cooee, again. We found Auntie Sarah with a blanket around her shoulders wet through. She had got off the track and was trembling all over. We took her back to her tent. Auntie Sarah's tent was dry so we didn't know why she left it. It was up a little hill and she had a big fire going outside. We put dry clothes on her and the men built up the fire. We stayed there all night.

It was a flood all right.

ELDERLY GENTLEMEN

Mr Frank Boyes left Robertdale and built a hut in the bush at North East River. He was a great age. He would cut wood and pile it up for when he got old. He used to talk to himself. Mr Jack Gardner, who kept the store at Lughrata, would bring food up to him, and another man, Mr Wattie Archer, who lived alongside for a while. This man was brother to Mr Archer on Cape Barren Island and he died before Mr Boyes. They lived like hermits, but you were always sure of cup of tea when you called there. The Robinsons from Five-Mile used to take a short cut from Five-Mile to see these elderly gentlemen. Frank and George Boyes were well educated. Mr Frank was the best. He had a wireless and would argue with the men on the wireless and tell them that they were wrong.

We were going down the road, Mum and I—our wireless was broken at the old home so we had to go down to Esme's to hear the serial, 'It Walks by Night'. There were gum-tree roots all over the road. It was a dark night and I had my hand around Mum's arm. The torch wasn't very good because the batteries were nearly out. I said to her, 'Jump'. She said, 'what are you jumping for?' I said, 'There's an extra gum root on the road'. I said, 'I think it's a snake. At certain times they travel of a night'. So we jumped and we turned around to have a look. When we put the torch on it, it was moving. We kind of knew how many gum roots there were on the road—so there was always these stories.

COOKING

Mutton birds can be cooked several different ways. We used to make a brown stew in the old iron pots. There is grilled mutton-birds, fried mutton-birds, baked mutton-birds with onions and stuffing, curried mutton birds with rice, sea pie, and salted birds.

For smoked mutton-birds we used to thread the birds on a stick and put them over a drum and keep the fire in the drum for four to six weeks.

We made kangaroo tail soup and brawn. We would dip the kangaroo tails in hot water and scrap the skin off.

We had coupons to buy meat, sugar, tea, butter and clothes. We made our own soap out of dripping and we used mutton-bird oil for rubbing our chests for flu. Garlic in your shoes was a remedy for whooping cough. We would boil the buzzies from the vine of the bush and bottle. We ate grass tree bread which is the meat of the tree—white in colour and sweet in taste. We loved it.

All my people cooked fruit cakes with mutton-bird fat dripping. The women were good cooks.

They used to cook bread, damper and johnny cake in bakers [camp ovens]. Uncle Bun Beeton used to make his damson jam in the baker. Uncle Bun used to have an orchard at Pinescrub which had peaches, damson, grapes and a vegetable garden. On my school holidays I used to stay with Johnny Maynard, his wife Nellie and their children, Hazel, Phillip, and Ruby. They lived on top of the hill at Pinescrub. They had a cow which was the best I have seen for producing cream. They would boil the milk and skim the cream off it. Nellie used to make butter, but it was just about butter before we started. We used to take it to the salt water to wash it. When we cooked our crayfish we put them straight into boiling water—all Aboriginal people do it that way.

One of the prettiest sights I ever saw in my life was in about 1937, on my first trip out to Babel Island. As I was going past Cat Island I saw it smothered with lovely white gannets. It was a picture. The last time I was out at Babel there were only a few there. It's a shame seeing these lovely white birds disappearing but it was a sight to see when the island was full of them.

Cat Island is one of the few breeding sites of the Australian Gannet in Australia. The other sites are Black Pyramid Island in north west Tasmania, Pedro Branca and Eddystone Rock in southern Tasmania, and two small colonies off the Victorian coast.

The Cat Island gannetry, once the largest in Australia, with up to 5000 birds nesting on two acres (0.8 hectares) in 1908, is now the smallest, due mainly to human depredation and vandalism. Free of disturbance, there is hope that the colony will increase to a viable size.

Matthew Flinders and George Bass were probably the first to see the colony when Bass landed there in 1798. He brought back a boat load of seals and gannets. The naturalist societies held several annual camp-outs in the Furneaux Group in the 1890's and early this century. They would hire a steamer and, with a spirit of adventure, set out on their trips, the highlight of which was to see the gannets of Cat Island.

Guano was mined on the Island until about 1925 but this does not seem to have had much effect on nesting. For several years before the Second World War the Tasmania Fauna Board stationed a warden, Bill Riddle, on the island to watch over the birds. In the 1938–39 season, 1000 chicks were raised. The decline in numbers began during the War and was most severe over the period from about 1940 to 1951. The decline has continued and the colony is now near extinction. Shooting of adults and taking of chicks for bait is believed to have been the main reason.

Cat Island is readily accessible from Lady Barron, and abalone divers work nearby. Fishing boats shelter from storms in the lee of the island. We can all help the gannets build up their numbers. Visitors to the colony should approach it quietly and leave within a short time. It is the responsibility of everyone to protect the gannets. Bait other than gannets and other sea birds is readily available. Gannets breed in the summer and birds feeding at sea may be catching food for their young. Happily, it seems that little depredation by man has occurred in recent years. In Great Britain a colony of gannets increased from only fifteen pairs in 1875 to several thousands of birds one hundred years later. Let's look after our gannets on Cat Island and see them return to their former glory.

Island News, Flinders Island, 23 March 1979

MAKING DO

When the grass-tree dried you could break off the bits and pieces. This was used for furniture varnish. It was sold to America after the Second World War for this purpose.

Brushes and brooms were made from tussock grass—they were used to white-wash fireplace bricks after they became black after wood fires. This was done once a week. Brooms were also made from tea-tree, for sweeping wooden floors. They were tied together with string and were made when the tree was green and bushy.

Moccasins were made from kangaroo [wallaby] skins, the fur side to the foot and skin side on the outer. Laces were made from the skin when the fur was cut off.

Poultices for skin inflammations were made from sugar, Velvet soap and nut-brown soap. The heated poultice was placed on the skin.

When rusty nails were caught in the feet, the feet were battered with a butter batter. This was done hard, to force the poison out of the injury.

Sponges from the beach were used for kitchen cleaning, and pots were cleaned with ashes.

Chapter three
Memories

It's been a long time since I tried to get this book together, about nine years in all. Things would come to me about the people on the island, my people. I can remember my Aunty Celia and Grannie Rebecca, when they were very sick. Grandfather had to take them away to Scottsdale Hospital in the boat. Aunty Celia was dying of TB when she went over, but I don't know what was wrong with Grandma. She was on the mend until she fell in the bath, so she passed away too, a fortnight between the both of them, with Aunty Celia dying first. They had a lot of sickness at those times. When they were told they had TB most of them died of fright because there seemed to be no cure. They used to fret about it and never liked to go to the hospital.

My grandfather, Neuto Everett, used to do a little tin mining, not much, but his real masterpiece was playing music—accordions, violins, he could play any kind of music and he'd always be there to help in sickness if someone wanted any help. He'd always go to find out if they wanted someone to sit up for a night with the sick. There was no hospital on Flinders Island to put them in until later years, when we got the bush nursing sisters and later the hospital. It was never easy for the people on the islands. In that first aid kit there'd only be castor oil, better known as a 'blue bottle', a fair number of Aspros, Epsom Salts, and different herbs which they made and used themselves. They always had their Epsom Salts, taken in morning. My mother used to take it at night.

It was always lovely to go for a walk, or watch the moonlight, or the full moon coming up. There always seemed to be plenty of time to study the moon, stars, skies, clouds. Sit on the hill and watch the seas, the gales—to watch the great big seas and in the end there'd be low water—to watch the tides go out and bring up a lot of shells. There doesn't seem to be the shells there now at Flinders.

When I used to stay at Pinescrub with Johnny Maynard and family he used to ride a white horse home every week from the Five-Mile where he worked. Mrs Johnny would sit on a chair on the verandah looking over the hill and she'd say Johnny's coming now and I'd say, 'My word, he's a long time coming up the road', and she could see him just coming out of the honeysuckle scrub. That was miles before he got to the main road. But she knew when to put the kettle on to have his meal ready for him. She could always look down to see him coming through this one place. They seem to be able to see a long way away.

We also had a boy with us at Killiecrankie, although he's dead now, and he could see bullfrogs in the dark. I think they could see in the dark. He'd go and pick up all these bullfrogs and he'd carry them home.

Uncle Bun always seemed to be around when there was trouble. If someone was sick he would come over with fruit from his orchard. Uncle Charlie Jones had a horse called Edna, she was a thoroughbred. Charlie didn't seem to know how to ride her and many a time she'd throw him, but he was always game enough to go back and get on again. There was one time when he was galloping down the road behind Mr Barry in his ute, who used to bring the children to school. Edna went so fast that she bucked and threw Charlie right into the back of the ute. Mr Barry didn't know Charlie was there till he got back to the shop.

There would be dancing at Pinescrub and all the people from Robertdale would attend. Mum and Dad and the children would walk home again to Robertdale or later across the hills to Killiecrankie. We'd do it all over again because they were better times then than they are today. Mr Dickie Smith used to come to the dances and he'd have the bowyangs on. He always put his knee up before he started the polka, till the player that played the accordion got on the right note, and then he'd put his foot down and around the floor he'd go. They were all good old-time dancers.

Mr Johnny Maynard used to MC the square dances and we had to do them properly, too.

Then we played cricket with a rubber ball and I would bowl underarm. Rounders, too, was our game. We used to practise dancing in the house at Robertdale and we would cut up candles and put them on the floor to make it slippery. This time we thought we'd get some mutton-bird oil, or the dripping down, and put on the floor. After the first lot we put down we knew we had made one great big mistake, so we got ashes and scrubbing brushes, we scrubbed all the floor out before Mum came home.

Morton Maynard, the carpenter, who built houses for us, went to Chappell Island mutton-birding and was bitten by a snake. They used to say you'd die straight away from fright. Some laughed about it, but Mr Eric Worrell said that with some snakes on Chappell, if you were bitten in the right place you could die on the spot, so that wasn't very nice.

I can remember when the men folk had finished work at the week-end, they would always be whittling with the pocket knife, making little boats out of wood. They used to make many things. They were always doing something with their hands—whittling wood, making nets, mending nets with shuttles, and plaiting leather. As children we would plait grass tussocks and tie them together across the track. People would fall over them, but we got the stick for doing that. There were many things I can remember doing with the reeds and grass, like making mat rugs and baskets. Today we still have some of our men and women folk who can do whittling and weaving and make many things. We still have to get our knowledge of arts and craft together to pass down the little bits of culture that was given to us by our parents—like shell-necklace making, whittling, weaving and story-telling.

We drank mutton-bird oil. If you drink too much it will come out through your skin, but its good for your lungs. It used to be rubbed into our chests when we were children, mixed with some camphorated oil or wild garlic. We had to live the white man's way, the white women's way, which hasn't been any disgrace to us. We had to learn both ways, more so than the whites because we had to live with white people. I only wish I could have learnt more about our own culture. Some of that has come back to us, and we're not ashamed of it now. We can hold our heads high, and we can try to live both ways as much as we can. I know a lot people on both sides. In recent years I've not been to the mutton bird islands, but I did to get over to Trefoil in 1981 for a day trip.

Another time we left the west beach at Babel in a motor boat—it was coming up to blow, we had to get away. We were going out to the trading vessel, *Margaret Thwaites*. One of the birders counted up his family and found that one boy was missing. Something told us to look around to the north point, and there he was. So they put us aboard, and had to go back to shore to get this boy. His father had to count all his children up, he had a fair few in the family so we were lucky that he wasn't a long way out to sea before he missed him. This is part of mutton birding. You always had to count up your children before you left these isolated islands, so there wouldn't be anyone left there. The children used to cook mutton-bird hearts on a stick, they'd shrivel up on the stick, as long as they were cooked properly they were lovely.

There's always been those from other parts of the world who come to write about the people of Aboriginal descent on the Straits islands. They haven't been passive in what they've said. Ever since I was a girl there has been government officials visiting but they never got any stories from my people.

Uncle Johnny Smith and Aunty Millie were living at Robertdale when an official went up there to see them. Uncle Johnny Smith and Aunt Millie sat down. 'They won't get anything from me', he said, and they didn't. I don't blame him. Such a lot of people like the police, the councillors, the wardens all stand up and ask for our history but if they stopped to think, they have one too. Perhaps they don't want that put in books, either.

God gave us eyes, and a tongue, and I've always been brought up to believe that the blacker you are the quicker you are in the eye—very alert in the eye. And so we are, we have seen more than people think we have. We're not dumb-dumbs all together.

It's not been easy for me as I haven't got the education to get a lot done, but there are always things in the old mind, and there are bits and pieces that have been given to me by a lot of people who have been very helpful—even the ones that can't write. It's marvellous what you can get from someone who you don't expect to know some history of our people. The main thing is not to let anyone put anything over you. That's why you must learn to read and write, learn to count money, get a ready reckoner or something, and count money as you've never counted before. Learn such a lot, because of what's put over my people years ago, when they couldn't read nor write.

I've learnt a lot and I'm still learning although I'm getting up in years. Things are still coming to me or someone brings me something and I can learn more. You can meet up with some good white people who can be very good to help us. They can see fairness in everything. It makes it very hard for them too I suppose, but we are getting through and I think they all make some headway. It's right what I say. The young people can go further and they seem to be a lot better in getting things across—using a lot of jaw breakers, a lot of big words. That's good for them. They would have to speak to me in plain Australian, but it's good for them to learn these words, because this is what they need in years to come, and to get to know what they are talking about.

Yes, it's going to be a long time before we all can be on even terms with the Europeans, not that we want to be any better but just so we can speak and try to do our work and have our own land. Those who want to live out in the country can grow their gardens, milk the cows or ride their horses. It probably won't be in my time but things are changing, the world's changing and so are the people in it. The world is not as large as people think it is, in fact it is becoming very small so that people can mix together. A cousin has been very good—a very proud woman. She gave a talk in her kitchen one day while I was there, she brought tears to me eyes. She's a few years older then me but her memory is still very good. Other writers have used Bonwick's books as a reference, and have got something out of it, they can switch it or twist it anyway they want to.

My sister, Girlie, left it too long when in labour with one of her children. There was a storm, rain and wind, and they had to rouse a brother-in-law to take my sister down. He got the old car going and he said his prayers from Killiecrankie to Whitemark to keep the car going. They just got there in time. There used to be a lot of babies which just got to the hospital. Mrs Victor Beeton was another one, way out at some place on the east coast of Flinders. Mum told Dad that he'd better go and see how Ivy was getting on as Victor was away up at Badger. Dad just got there and Ivy said she wasn't going to stop there any longer because she thought she'd better get to the hospital. Dad said he knew she had to go, but we had to make her comfortable on the old horse and cart as the road was rough. So we got an old mattress and an old chair and we set her up on this chair till we got down to our home. Eventually we saw the bush nurse come up to see Ivy. She was a grand woman, Sister Blundstone. What she had to put up with way out in the never-nevers.

Jim Boy Maynard (left) who served in the Great War shaking hands with his brother, Jack Maynard, who served in World War II.

My people mentioned below went and fought in the wars. 'Dummy' (Goodson) Armstrong (died on the Burma railway) Walter Beeton, J. Maynard, I. Mansell, C. Maynard, H. Burgess, L. Maynard, Three Gore Brothers, James Maynard, Tommy Mansell, young Tommy Mansell, Lionel Brown, Ken Mansell, A.J. Delphin, Thelma Norman Maynard, Bob Everett, Jeff Everett and Tom Riley, J.H.P. Maynard and probably a lot more that I don't know about.

George Mansell who served in the Great War.

Alan Burgess who served in the Great War

THE GREAT WAR

These men died of wounds, were killed in action, died on service or went to War. This is from the memorial on Cape Barren Island.

A.D. Mansell	W. Mansell	G.E. Brown	G. Fisher
G.E. Mansell	V. Mansell	F.W. Brown	W. Brown
M. Mansell	W. Mansell	H.C. Brown	
T. Mansell	G.W.L. Mansell	M.B. Brown	
J.H. Mansell	A.M. Burgess Sr.	J.C. Brown	

Vince and Leedham Maynard who served in World War II.

51

WORLD WAR II

A lot of our men went to the wars, some were killed, some came home very sick from the poisonous gas used in the war.

Viv Maynard	Mark West
Norman West	Freddie Brown
Russell Beeton	Phillip Holt
Owen Armstrong	Clive Beeton
Mervyn West on road to Burma	V. Green
George West on road to Burma	Ken Everett
Bob Everett on road to Burma	L. Brown
C. Maynard (Williams)	B. Maynard
Jeff Everett	V. Maynard

Desmond Mallett, James Everett, and a lot more of my people went to the Vietnam War. Those who didn't go overseas joined the Militia.

RESERVE ON CAPE BARREN ISLAND

At one time there was a reserve on Cape Barren Island. This reserve was for all half-castes. The only people allowed on this reserve were the Aboriginal people on the Cape Barren Reserve poll. One evening Girlie, her husband, Tim, my husband, Markie and I were walking down the road towards the Corner. The schoolteacher came up and asked us where we were going, what we were doing, how long we were staying and just about everything else. He even asked if we belonged there. He told us we had to be off the reserve before dusk and to come back the next morning. We were spending Christmas with our cousin Andrew and Gran' aunt Mary Maynard. Andrew had to talk to this man as he had never talked before. Finally this man let us stay there until the New Year.

At Cape Barren Island my people weren't allowed to drink on the reserve or drink in the hotel at Whitemark on Flinders Island. Alcohol used to be bought for them. Then just about the time when the Second World War started they opened it up for the Aborigines to go to the hotel. I was having a drink at the

Funeral service at the church on Cape Barren Island.

Boats built by Bill Brown, my great great grandfather, photographed at The Corner, Cape Barren Island.

Whitemark Hotel with the late Hubert Maynard and I said, 'No one plays up now'. He said, 'It is because we can come and get our drink when we want to'. It was strange before. They couldn't get a drink and if someone got it for them and there was a fight, it wouldn't matter who started it—it was only the black man who would get locked up in the jail at Whitemark. Some white men, when they got sober, would go and bail them out. If there was only one locked up they would bail him out and pay the fine.

A cousin and I were at a hotel in Launceston minding our own business when some people came in and one man said, 'Wherever you look you see black crows'. I heard it, my cousin didn't, but a friend with him said, 'There is only one black crow and that's you', she put him in his place—some people are as ignorant as the pigs on Schouten Hill. Some single people who came to Flinders were told not to marry half-caste men or women by some of the ignorant people of the island. One young man who came over to Flinders to work at the stud farm at Kentdale was told he mustn't marry a half-caste, and that there were three other classes of people living on Flinders Island. One day I was going along to the shop and I saw him coming, I opened the gate and he said something to me about the different classes of people living on Flinders Island and he called them the big head, and the middle class and the poorer class, then the half-caste, and I said 'Yes and I'm the half-caste'. He just about fell off his horse. People don't stop to think when they say these things to people.

I know of one family who used to say this, I don't know why. Maybe it was because their own sister married an Aborigine. Probably that was why.

I think now and am proud of what we are and our talent. I can remember a girl working at Paton and Baldwin's in Launceston with her friend, a white girl. She liked black people all right but she also said, 'They always looked dirty to me'.

Well its been a long story and probably still no end to it, but we are not afraid to think ourselves as good as the next one. Its been hard but we'll all get there. Some people think we don't know anything, probably we don't, but we still have feelings and love people, love our religion, our Saviour. We're not greedy, but I am afraid some of them will be before very much longer because they're learning greedy ways. The more money you get, the more you want. There'll never be any happiness where there are greedy people. There is no love—no-one to give into people, no one to help one another in sickness. Money—you're no good without it, but you're no good with it.

I think that my great grandmother was Jane Foster, a part-Aboriginal. She was at Cape Portland but we were told something different all together. I have a feeling I know the reason why we get told these things, there is more to it than meets the eye. Great-grandpa Armstrong, a Scot, came from Cape Portland and he met Jane there. Their children had blue eyes and they were brought up properly, table manners, grace, and said their prayers at night. Aunty Mary Maynard, Jane's daughter, was always praying to our Lord, when we stayed with her we had to sit up straight at the table and try to use our knife and fork properly. They must have had that upbringing from somewhere. Some of our people try to look for a history. They say one thing, then they tell us another, just to get us off the beaten track. We're not all as silly as we look. Two years ago I went to Cape Portland and went down to the old Foster home as there is always some feeling there. I picked up two Aboriginal stones. There is something that tells you which is the right stone. After an early massacre a little girl was found but she could only say that her name was Amanda so, Portland being the area, they named her Amanda Portland. I went to Cape Portland and it is a beautiful place, and from there I could see the islands, right across, nice beaches.

I went to see about history at Derby, I was told you have to have identification, know what you're looking for. I was told that to trace back you have to pay because a lot of people have been there asking for information about someone else's relations. It's not right to then go away and scandalise someone. So its a lot harder now to get things way back in the 1830s. I learnt of names while I was up there, a lot of Aboriginal names, even Conara which we pass when we come and go to Launceston.

My daughter, Lenna, was reading history, she went down to the library at Burnie and came home with all these Tasmanian Aboriginal history books, she found one and she was reading out to me about soldiers and the red-coats when they shot the

Aborigines down at Jerico, somewhere near the Three Thumbs Hills. Before they got them our brave men took thirty soldiers and red coats with their spears. They were a pretty brave lot that tribe at Jerico. A lot of people today destroy things and leave their rubbish lying all about, but our old Aborigines never wasted anything. We were brought up to just get enough to eat and then go out and get another lot. We never got food to waste. My father, when he wanted a duck, went out and shot one.

People used to try to get you to go to church, to be a Christian as they call it. But the funny thing about it is it makes you hard. They don't consider that you were brought up to believe in our Lord, my Lord as well as theirs. Relations on both sides of the family made us go to church to be good like them, but it makes you laugh, because we believe anyway.

Where we hunted we built. We've had land and we still love the land. It has not always been sold over a bottle of wine.

I went to Cape Barren in recent years. I don't think I could live there—I don't know whether at my age now I could live by myself, but if I was young, just got married, well I'd rather be living at a isolated place like the islands where you can get away from the rat race. I think its wonderful to go back to those places for a holiday, to live in a tent, watch the tide, listen to the waves coming in, the tide going out, the wind coming up in the sea. It looks very cruel sometimes but in the most lovely weather its beautiful. Then you walk along the beaches and collect shellfish.

Years ago people said that if you didn't sow and plough your land, you couldn't own it and therefore you couldn't eat shellfish. It's marvellous what excuses people get up. There wasn't that much to do in those times, only hunt and work the land, sow the seed, cut the ferns until they got a horse to plough—then you made fences, and anyone could do that. I used to go away to cut some posts. We cut a tree down once, but before the tree fell my brother didn't sing out to lunge sideways. I lunged straight out in front of it and the branches knocked me flat to the ground. I could have been killed.

I love every little island in the Straits. To see all the beautiful calm water and the fishing boats, or a trading vessel going across. Boats everywhere and a stone lighthouse. It is sometimes very calm around there, but of course it's not always calm, it's often rough. I don't think I could live inland. It always seems as though I'm not getting enough fresh air, as I've been born and bred near the water, the salt water all around me. I suppose its just what you get used to.

I went through the ladies jail out at Bridgewater. I've been there twice to see what they went through. They have dummies of the red coats and convicts. I asked the gentlemen who runs it who caused the trouble, as if I didn't know, but I thought I better ask again.

We used to go to dances sometimes. At one dance Girlie got up with one of her own people, it was a barn dance. The white people just fell out—they wouldn't dance, and when Girlie and her partner sat down they started again. One of the white islanders, Landon Woods, came and got Girlie to get up, to see if they would fall out again, but they didn't.

THE HALF-CASTES

Women Concerned—Segregation Supported

The opinion of the women in the AWNI acording to a deputation which waited upon the Chief Secretary (Mr Caulde James) yesterday, is that the Government should at once tackle the problem of the half-castes on Cape Barren Island. They consider that if the inhabitants of the settlement were brought to Tasmania and dispersed an unsatisfactory situation would be created.

The deputation, which represented the northern division of the AWNI of Tasmania, was introduced by Mr. J. F. Ockerby, MHA.

Mrs V. Ransom, Windermere, said that at the last meeting of the league in Launceston, it had been resolved that the Premier should be approached and urged to take some action to ameliorate the conditions of the whole of the half-castes, but especially of the women and children, before the position became quite hopeless. The problem had become a very serious one, and it was essential that something should be done regarding medical, domestic and occupational instruction.

The fact of the strong moral obligation that developed upon the community to do something to make the children safer and happier was stressed by Mrs C. Evans.

Mrs F.G. Dougharty said that as things were at present there was no hope for the young people on the settlement. She was convinced that the half-castes must remain segregated as a self-contained community, and that some constructive policy should be enunciated and carried out. Such a policy was lacking at the moment. If the Government did not know what to do, the opinion of expert authorities should be obtained. It should surely be possible for the people on the island to grow their own food stuffs and make their own clothes. Recent reports were very disquieting.

Mr James—They are grossly exaggerated.

It seemed, Mrs Dougharty added, that the best solution would be the handing over of the settlement to somebody like the Australian Inland Mission.

This view was supported by Mrs R. McNair, who believed that under proper control and instruction, the people would be happier and more prosperous.

In his reply, Mr James said that conditions on the island were not as bad as had been made out. The conditions of life compared unfavourably with those of the white race, but the mistake had been made when the half-castes had been sent to the island, and he was not convinced that the remedy lay not in concentration, but in dissipation. The inhabitants of the settlement had become indolent and shiftless, but the men had shown themselves excellent workers, and trouble had arisen because of the isolation and consequent inbreeding. He had secured a report from Mr N. Hawkins who was in charge of the island to the effect that conditions were not so bad as had been stated. The unfortunate stirring up of the trouble had been responsible for the new outcry. The problem reared its head only when a member of Parliamant went to the island.

The Government was not taking its responsibility lightly. It recognised a distinct moral responsibility but was satisfied that concentration must end. The Board of Inland Missions had recommended breaking up the settlement. The people were *perfectly happy and quite contented but they were not susceptible to training. The children were educable to a certain degree. The trouble arose when they left school and had no chance of getting into industry, or in to any profitable occupation. Gradual absorption in the general Tasmanian community would solve the whole problem and indeed if any of the residents of the settlement wished to leave the island they were perfectly at liberty to do so. Mrs Evans objected that the introduction of a number of people with low standards into the community would have a bad moral effect, but Mr James urged that there would be little danger of any unhappy developments. The only chance the half-castes had was of becoming units in the Tasmanian community.*

(Source and date unknown)

CAPE BARREN ISLAND

Years ago when the Labor Party was in power, in Major Davies' time, an unemployment benefit was given to the unemployed for the first time. My Grandparents from Cape Barren were boat builders and built their own houses and made coffins. I feel that the government should have given money to train the young people on the Island to carry on the boatbuilding and other things. I feel that the pride and dignity of my people was once again taken away from them when this happened.

MUTTON-BIRDING ON BABEL AND CHAPPELL ISLANDS

In the beginning of the mutton-bird season in November the strong winds come and the old birds come in. At the end of the season in April the strong wind comes again to take away the young birds.

When we got to the islands the men would get the wood and the women helped to clean out the sheds, whitewash them inside. Some had cement floors and in some you put tussock grass down. We had to go up the hill and cut the grass with a reap hook, carry it down to the sheds and put on the floor. The main shed had racks around the wall so that when the birds were cleaned, before they were opened, they could be put on the racks to cool. The trading boats would bring the barrels and salt. The salt was used for salting the birds and the barrels for the birds when they were cleaned and salted. When birding starts the men go out to the rookeries and get the birds and put them on a spit, a long stick. They carry them to the shed, put the spit on a rack, then take them off and squeeze the oil out of the bird into a gurry pot. The oil is squeezed out through their beaks. The birds were then put through the hole in the plucking house, which was made like a lean too. A man would pluck or a woman and a child would cut their legs off then they were put through the cleaning part of the shed. The cleaning part of the shed had the scalding pot, the cleaners would be sitting around ready waiting for the birds. While they were hot we dipped the birds in the hot water, then put them on bags which we had spread out over our laps and brushed the down off the birds. They were then put through another hole in the wall to be laid out on the racks to cool. Then they were opened and salted and put into the barrels. When the barrels were full they rolled them out onto the sand banks near the beach. But not all the sheds were by the beach.

We would get a bucket of water and put the salt in and a potato. When the potato sank we would put more salt in until the potato floated. We then poured the water into the barrel through the bung hole, we would check through the bung hole to make sure the birds were all right. The men rolled the barrels down the bank and then took them right out to the motor boat. The men in the boat would put a board down so the barrel could be rolled up into the boat. The men would be wet all day until they finally got all the barrels out to the motor boat. The motor boat would then go to a trading boat like the *Shearwater*, *Margaret Thwaites*, *Lady Flinders* or the *Lady Jean*. Launceston was their destination.

Mr and Mrs Nichols of Stanley knew the islands like the palm of their hands. Women were not allowed to salt the birds when menstruating. We had to tell the boss's wife and we were given other jobs, like looking after other womens children, laying fresh grass on the floors or looking after tea. We also carried up salt water to scrub the stone floors and scattered sand on the toilet floors, the doors were made of chaff bags. The feathers were

Mutton-bird chick.

bagged up to be sent away and made into pillows and bed mattresses. There was a mutton-bird inspector who had to inspect the conditions of the huts, toilets, sleeping quarters and the barrels but he never had much to complain about.

I used to salt mutton-birds. Some people reckon that in the old days they never did salt birds but just took the oil. However, they used salt from the rocks, I know because my father had no salt once and we couldn't wait for the boat. He went away and I went with him and we got salt from the rocks, a lot of salt for the meat. It lasted a long time. They just had to do it to survive.

After the birding we always had a dance at Whitemark, the Hospital Ball or something. You had to shampoo your hair, wash it two or three times before you could go to the dance. You never could get rid of the smell of the birds or the feathers. They used to bag the feathers up and sell them. They'd all have fun, jump all about in the feathers, which would get up your nose and restrict your breathing. We used to have dances on the grass floor out at Babel, but it didn't matter there because they were all mutton-birders and working at mutton-birding. No-one could smell mutton-birds because they were all the same.

The nursing sister used to come with us to dance at Babel and have Ted Burgess doing a clog-dance or playing the accordion with the old jigs, Irish jigs, Scottish reels. Violins, mouth organs, bones and spoons—they don't play them now. I don't know why—it's still in them to do it.

We would fish on Sundays for a change. We would usually catch blueheads as I can't catch flathead. We used to make soup. We were told by the old folk that we should only eat fish with scales on. I always have fish on Good Friday. It would be terrible—no butter, just jam, fish soup, fish boiled, boiled fish until after midnight then probably someone would start cooking mutton birds again, ready for a meal. Often we would go for our walks along the west beach at Babel to Sam Thomas', at West Point, Ucky Mansell, Edervine Mansell's father and his mother used to have their sheds there.

The shed on top of the hill was Victor Beeton's. Ivy Beeton used to work there and Millie Mansell. The children would play along the rocks. The women folk would come out and yell out to keep away from rocks and to get home. There's always such a lot to do and on top of that they had to keep an eye on the children in case they fell off the rocks. If they just played down in front of the beach it would be all right.

I was always pretty good at minding children. If they got cut with glass or got splinters in their feet (half of them wouldn't wear shoes or boots) or if they poisoned their foot. We'd always have to make poultices. We'd put castor oil on their foot and try to get it out while they were waiting for the doctor or the nurse to come. It would often be blowing and they couldn't get there. Later they got the sister to stay on the Island which was marvellous because we had some splendid sisters there.

And we'd go around to the Gulch which is like a little

township. There was a shop there. In the end they had a two-way radio and we would send the messages and the messages would come through from the police that the doctor was coming or they were coming.

We used to make our couches with palings and put grass in a chaff bag, to make a cushion right along it to make it soft. Sometimes because the camp ovens were heavy we would wait for some young folk to come in to help lift them down or lift them up. We would bake our own bread, do our washing at the weekend, do our ironing, only on the Saturday. We weren't allowed to wash and iron on Sunday. They brought us up so religious that we had to do everything on Saturday, ready for work on Monday.

RADIO

One time I had to look after the two-way radio. I had to make a call from where we were at the Gulch at Babel to the policeman at Lady Barron. My daughter showed me what to do and I finally got through with the message. Phyllis Jackson, whose job it was to work the radio had to go away on business, which was why I was there. Before that I always wanted to speak on the radio. I used to listen to the boats on a wireless we had. It really fascinated me.

BOATS

I was working on the west beach out at Babel, I had to go away to cut grass with the reap hook, and while I was way up the hill putting the grass in a chaff bag to bring down for the mutton-bird sheds, I looked out to sea, toward the North East River, and I saw something bobbing up and down in the water. I finished cutting the grass and then I came down to the mutton-bird shed, where I worked with Morton Green and Andrew Maynard. I told Andrew that the fishing boat was lying at the west beach and I said to him, do you know if their motor boat is lying around the other side of the boat. When he went along to West Point the boat was missing, so he and Morton got a little dinghy and they pulled out to the fishing boat. They had to go aboard, they didn't really know what to do but they pulled up anchor and they went to look for this boat. Sure enough it was there, two of the fishermen in the motor boat. The first thing they asked for was a cigarette. They had to thank Morton and Andrew for saving their lives.

You would be used to the fishing boats coming from the south-east beach around to the west beach. One of the first nights when I was out at Babel I lay awake, frightened of snakes crawling around the mutton-bird shed as someone had told that there was a snake the year before in the room that I was sleeping in. It was blowing a proper gale from the east and I could hear something coming. I couldn't make out what it was and then I heard the boat winch, so I knew it was a fishing boat coming around in the storm to lie at the west beach. It was the *Surprise*, one of the best boats that ever sailed the Bass Strait, and Mr Nolan, one of the best captains who ever was in a boat. He knew how to handle the *Surprise*.

A few years after that I was listening to the wireless, they'd be giving out sounds for people to guess, and it was months before someone had the right answer, and I thought to myself well it will be easy it is a boat winch. Because I didn't have the wrapper from a particular brand of soap to send in I couldn't join in. It was a long time before someone got the answer, it was a motor car that they won. I could have kicked myself ever since.

Another fishing boat, the little *Blanche*, had to take a sick boy from Babel into Lady Barron in bad weather, they didn't want him to go but he went and we were saying our prayers. Anyway a big fishing trawler which must have been on its way to New Zealand or somewhere must have spotted this little fishing boat and she came right in and went alongside the little boat, until she got through the Pot Boil. If someone was sick, well they just had to go whether it was blowing, whether they knew their boats could do it or not. They just went with these sick people.

My Grandfather's boat, the *Dora*, was built by Richard William (Dick) Davey, who married Rosina Lee, daughter of John and Bridget Lee. Davey came to the islands at the age of eighteen from Longford in Tasmania, perhaps to work for Robert Gardner at Settlement Point. Later he ran some sheep and cattle at Apple

Orchard on Cape Barren Island and did some boat building. The future Field Marshal Bernard Montgomery stayed with the Daveys at the Apple Orchard and played with their boys while his father, the Bishop of Tasmania, was visiting the island in 1890s. Richard Davey died in 1930 at the age of seventy-nine and Rosina in 1934 at the age of seventy-three.

My brother-in-law, Andy, and Markie, my husband, were in a boat called the *Phyllis* at Killiecrankie. They were up near Boat Harbour out near some sunken rocks and a gale came up. They had to get home as soon as they could. We were getting worried about them. My sister Esme went out to look for them on the water at Killiecrankie Point. Esme thought she could see something like a small boat. She screamed, we ran—myself and Terry Wheatley. But couldn't see anything that looked like a boat on the water as it was all covered with white heads. It wasn't very long before the *Phyllis* turned up near Killiecrankie Creek. Markie had taken his thigh boots and some clothes off. He said that if the sea broke on her we will be feeding the sharks. Andy had to keep the oil up to the engine.

Esme and her husband and their son Lionel went once to the Inner Sister on the launch *Albatross* to get mutton birds. On the way back the launch started to leak. My sister was steering, Andy and Lionel had to bail till they got to Killiecrankie. Esme talked in her sleep all night about the boat sinking and about herself steering.

Silas Mansell helped Lou Baily and Dan Daniels in the police launch. They were good men in a boat. They used to go out to Babel and Cape Barren and other small islands.

Darrell, Lenna and Phyllis Jackson were working with me during the mutton-bird season at the Gulch on Babel Island. I was cleaning the birds with Nellie Maynard, Leedham Maynard, and 'Boof' Barry. Lenna and Darrell were cutting off the mutton bird legs. The *Shearwater* was loading casks of birds onto the boat. A young fellow came up to Phyllis—Darrell liked him and followed him down to the boat. Darrell went swimming and he was right under where the casks were going up into the boat. A cask of birds slipped off the winch. Big Buck Rooke yelled to Darrell to get away as quick as he could. The cask fell into the water, Darrell was underneath it. The men had gone ashore for more birds, they were on the beach. I didn't know that Darrell was down there. The men were silent, and they decided that someone would have to tell Ida her boy was gone. Les Jackson said, 'I will. I have known her all my life'. He had just started up to tell me when they saw Darrell over on Gulch Point. They didn't know that anyone could stay under water for so long. He would always stay under water for far too long before he came up.

GRANDFATHER ARMSTRONG'S BOAT

Grandfather Armstrong, who is buried across the creek at Killiecrankie, had a boat called the *Dora*. She was thirty feet on the keel and had a ten foot beam. I was told Dad sold the *Dora* to a policeman called Riddle for seventy pounds. When Mr Riddle died the boat went to young Bill Riddle, who later sold her to Uncle Clem Beeton and later she was wrecked on Badger Island. Dad also had a dinghy called the *Possum Fat* which he used to row up and down the creek at Killiecrankie, getting his morning kindling sticks. It must have been an interesting life. Dad and other men used to make and mend nets. Grandfather Armstrong in his boat *Dora* took Mum, when she was going to have my brother Owen, over to the doctor in Launceston. Dad and Mum were waiting with Grandfather at Whitemark for the gale to go down. The steamer *Toroa* was there also. The glass was going up, but there was a big sea and it was still blowing. *Toroa* pulled out and sailed to Launceston. Dad wasn't any good in a boat, neither was Mum, but Grandfather was fine. The *Toroa* was a steamer, a lot bigger than the *Dora*. When the *Toroa* got to Low Head the *Dora* was there too. Grandfather was swearing at Dad and Mum was crying. She said the *Dora* was under water all way from Flinders Island. They only had sails.

Another time, Uncle Clem Beeton had to take Auntie Sarah, in a small boat called *Nora*, to Cape Barren from Badger as Auntie Sarah was having a baby. They left it a bit late and it was blowing a gale. They had to get down to the nurse Mrs Burgess. All the people at Cape Barren were saying their prayers for them, but they were all right. Only Uncle Clem was in the boat with no other men to help him.

Another time I was at Lady Barron, my sister-in-law, Mary Jane, was very ill. Flo Green was up at Cape Barren, so we had to send for her to come to her sister. It started to blow. I was sorry I sent for her because if they came in a boat I was frightened they would get drowned. Flo said she went to where all the men were playing cards as there weren't many boats at that time at Cape Barren. Flo asked the men if one of them could take her to Mary. Everybody went quiet, they knew it was blowing a gale, a real storm. But one man got up and said, 'I'll take you, Flo'. That man was Archie Mansell. The small boat was called *Nona*, another man jumped up and said, 'I'll come with you Archie'. He was Darcy Maynard. Flo could have kissed them. I was waiting at Lady Barron with Uncle Ted. Mary was still very sick. I thought they couldn't get down as it was just white heads on the water. Shannon Mansell brought me a fish up (to cook for Mary) that he had caught from the boat lying at Lady Barron. I was sitting on the door step and I thought I saw something like a boat going to Yellow Beach. I didn't know what it was until they walked in the door. It was blowing too hard to get into the wharf.

In the book *Mission to the Islands* my Grandfather, Harry Armstrong, is mentioned—he used to take Canon Browning about in his boat the *Julia*.

Bill Holloway had a boat called the *Falcon* which he would take to Babel Island. He was out at Babel when my sister-in-law, Flo Green, took sick with one of her babies. It was blowing a gale—an easterly so they wouldn't go through the Pot Boil. They had to go westabout. Morton Flo's husband had to go too. I watched them go to the North East River point. The *Falcon* was all awash but they got there.

There's many a woman had to go off the bird islands in a hurry to have their babies and many babies were born on the small islands.

The boat *Doris Louise* was built by Bill Brown, my great great grandfather. She was down at Lady Barron rotting away, but now she's being done up, I believe.

I went out in a small fishing boat called the *Reliance* to West

The last boat built by Great Great Grandfather Brown.

End to get the cray pots. We camped at Tanners Bay. The crays were running. My children Lenna and Darrell were at school. They used to walk out to the Pinescrub turn-off to pick up the school bus. A car from Emita used to pick the children up at Killiecrankie and my children would walk home to Tanners Bay. Well, I was out with my husband Markie in the boat and we got the pots when it came on to blow. The wind came up, the tide turned, and we were in a rip, in between small islands. We lost the rudder. Markie had no control and I got hysterical. Markie had to smack me across the face, and said to keep a cool head. There was no time to get frightened, I was thinking we would get drowned or smashed on the rocks. I couldn't swim even though I've lived alongside salt water all my life, all I could do was float. Then I thought of the children coming home from school, no-one would be there. They would be wondering where their parents were. A straw broom was always kept on a boat. Markie said, 'Pass me the straw broom', and he tied it where the rudder was supposed to be, so that he could use it as a rudder. He managed to keep the boat from going onto the rocks. When we got out of the rip and were going down past Pinescrub heading for home I felt safe. I was glad to get home so I could be there when the children arrived. I thought I was never going to see them again. I felt after that, wives shouldn't go out in the boats when they lived in isolated places.

Mr T. Purdon from the Battery Point shipyards brought the timber on the *Surprise* (when she was a trading boat to Flinders Island) when they built the Ferguson Jetty at Whitemark. My people sailed boats and built boats and took guano to Launceston often to sell it.

The old sailors told the weather by the moon—they knew by the moon if there was a gale coming—the moon would be on its back, with streaky clouds.

TIDES

If people were very sick they would know by the tide if they were going to die or get better. Some people even went down to the beach to check the tide. If the tide was on the turn you would go either way, low water meant you were going to get better. High water, you were going to die.

FISHING BOATS

Dick Burgess and his son Bernard were on the Victorian fishing boat, the *Myrtle Burgess*, crayfishing. They were working at St Helens Point, Tasmania. I think that at this time Victorian fishing boats weren't allowed to fish in Tasmanian waters. The policeman's wife waved a handerchief at them and they thought that someone needed help. They went in the motor boat to see what the trouble was. The policeman came out from behind a rock and shot at the motor boat. Dick turned the boat around. The policeman shot at the boat even though he was supposed to shoot over their heads to stop them. Bernard got shot. His father took him to the nearest town, St Helens, but he died. It was very sad. I can remember something about it. Mum was crying. She knew young Bernard.

Darcy Maynard was on the boat the *Dauntless*, the captain was Bill McKay. The water bailiff went aboard to seize the boat but Bill wasn't going to let him take it. The baliff pulled a gun and Bill pulled his arm down or put his foot on his arm. Bullets went through the deck. Bill McKay threw him over the steering wheel of the *Dauntless* and the wheel broke. The *Dauntless* was brought to Hobart, the water baliff did his job—but our men were brave too. Soon after they opened up the waters on the Tasmanian coast to all fishing boats.

Once I went to Babel with Flo and Morton, Andrew Maynard and George Mansell in the *Eveline*. The boat had an engine but it wouldn't go. All the children were with us, and two dogs. The dogs were tied up to the mast just before we left. 'Strike me pink with a blue bag', George Mansell said. We got out to the Pot Boil and had two channels to choose from. We had to go out to the big channel. The wind came up and, my word, it blew, just as we turned to go through. Andrew put the main sail up but he never had it fixed up properly. Soon it blew down. So there was only the jib left, and Andrew started to panic. Flo and all the children were down in bed and I was up on deck I knew if I went down below I would be sick too. The wind was on the starboard side of the boat so George Mansell took over. He told me to get down below. If I didn't he was going to tie me to the mast with the dogs, because if I fell overboard he couldn't come after me. Down below I went. She was a very strong boat if Andrew had the main sail fixed up. Anyway she lay on her side. We made a record trip to Babel with only her jib up. She was a boat that liked a gale of wind. Andrew built her but it was George Mansell that took us there. The deck was all awash.

You can go on and on about the way these men handled their boats. I went up to see someone in hospital in Launceston, I think it was Auntie Jinny Jackson. She told me Jack Mansell was along in the men's ward. I went along to see him even though I didn't know him very well. He knew me when I came through the door. He said you're Harry Armstrong's daughter, and while I was there he told me about how grandfather Armstrong and he would sail the boats. He used to live, I think, at Boat Harbour or Barbers Beach, next to Killiecrankie. He died a couple of nights after that. He told me a lot about them sailing the boat, most of them were very good in boats.

There was a boat called the *Lady Fay* belonged to Walter Beeton on Badger Island. Women sailed boats too. The men took firewood up in their boats to the mutton-bird islands. George Davey built the *Lady Fay* for Uncle Walter Beeton, Molly's father, and later sold it to Ossie Brody. Mr George Blyth had a boat called the *Rosezada*. They anchored her in the North East River. We were staying at the North East River in Mr Cherry's house, he was an artist. We were coming home when I said to Dad, 'The *Rosezada* is going down the river with no-one on board'. We had a look for the dinghy and had pulled her out in the water when we heard someone cooeeing. It was Mr Gardner. He ran down to where we were and we all went out to the *Rosezada*. Dad had to row the dinghy as fast as he could as we had to get aboard. They had the engine locked up and the tiller. We could put the sail up and jib, but we had to use a broom for a tiller. We turned her around and took her back to her moorings. Mr Gardner also kept the store at Lughrata.

James Bonwick says in one of his books that sealers took Aboriginal women from the coast of Australia and even from New Zealand. In 1898 the Furneaux Islanders were described by Edward Stephens, the school teacher on Cape Barren Island. One of the islanders was John Smith, a half-caste Tasmanian, who was so strong he was often seen to leap from combing to combing on whale boats whilst holding a sack of flour under his arm. Stephens found the islanders to be secretive, having apparently been taught from birth to answer, 'I don't know', to every question.

They had even lost all knowledge of Tasmanian custom.

HEALTH AND ABORIGINAL MIDWIVES

My mother and other women always kept a basin and their best towel for the doctor. There was only one doctor on Flinders Island and to my people he was a king. No-one was allowed to use the basin or towel, only the doctor and the bush nurse. She was like a queen. Our nurse, or sister, could ride a horse and bike as they had to rough it out on the bird islands. They had a guide to take them around the mutton-bird islands. The nurse had a house at Babel Island. I took the towel one day at home and dried my hands on it and I got the strap across the legs from Mum. Mrs Julie Burgess, Auntie Emma Maynard, Gussie Maynard and Betsy Maynard, were our midwives. They brought Aboriginal babies into the world and also white children. Maudie Brown took over after Mrs Burgess.

Mrs Alfred Stackhouse sr. was very good when you were sick.

Chapter four
Songs and sadness

INFLUENZA OUTBREAK

Uncle Alex Maynard, John Thomas, Uncle Tom Armstrong, Bill Brown, Auntie Myrtle Smith, Uncle Tas Smith, Len Mansell and Emilly Mansell. When they had heavy flu a lot of my people passed away. As far as I can remember we had splendid undertakers on Cape Barren Island who built the coffins in their own backyards. They had to bury about four a week and it was only a small place. They had to bury members of their families. They were very brave men. The coffins weren't anything to look at but they were very strong. My grandfather, Neuto Everett, and Andrew Maynard did a lot to help the sick. It didn't matter what you were dying of, there was no hospital, and only one doctor. So they had to take care of their sick, and a lot of others did the same. Andrew and Affie Maynard helped them out. They used to go in a horse and cart to bury our people but they never complained. At one time they even had to walk. Grandfather Neuto should have been a male nurse. Mrs May Jackson helped us when Dad was sick. She took me and Girlie to live with them. There was a time when some officials and press asked her to tell them about Flinders Island half-castes. She told them she wasn't going to tell

From left: Morton Green, Aunty Mary Armstrong Maynard, Louise Brown, Willie Green, Pearl Maynard, Andrew Maynard, and Vern Green.

them anything. 'Because', she said, 'Don't forget, they know as much about us Europeans as we do about them'.

We used to wash by hand. Sometimes I think it's cleaner because you put more elbow grease into it. The old braces that the men used to wear would have to be scrubbed too, as well as aprons, bags and mats. We used to dye the bags for mats. I would scrub the floor and it would be so clean you could have your meal on it. I often think about carpets. They're not clean, you know. You run a vacuum over them but still they don't get wiped until you bring the carpet man in and that's probably every two years or whenever you can afford it. But it's still not like the old floor. You used to get down there and scrub it with cold water because it made it whiter. I did the tables which had really white, beautiful boards. I used ashes for sandsoap, with a sponge from the beach. You don't get many sponges now. I have one now from Flinders Island. They used to come up a lot, stiff sponges, you could use them as scrubbing brushes.

ABORIGINAL WORDS

Mumlie pegs (lower part of plant left after cleaning scrub), Bidgie-widgies (burrs), Kanie gon (pig face), Ne Na (end of prayer, Amen or 'to you'), boobyalla, lilypea, (babyfood).

Aborigines used to eat sorrell for their greens. I have some growing and I used to eat it myself. I still have some, it tastes sour but it is good to eat. They say the cows like to eat it too.

With buzzy or burrs, the nobs are boiled up and you drink it. They boil it up and bottle it and keep cork tops in the bottle. It will keep for a month until it is ready to drink. It is very nasty to drink. Uncle Walter Beeton used to take this, he lived to a great age. He never had any sickness. He reckoned it purified the blood and stopped boils.

SONGS AND JOKES

Jim Boy Maynard said to Uncle Clarence Brown, who was deaf, that the Germans were getting closer. 'Yes', said Uncle Clarence, 'the turkeys are just over the hill'.

My mother Ivy Armstrong when she came to Launceston to live rang for a taxi. The man said, 'Where do you live?' and she said, 'Never you mind young man, just come at once'.

Grandma Rebecca was talking to Uncle George and Uncle Clem when they were only little boys. One said, 'What is ham?' Grandma Rebecca said, 'You silly fools, ham is a bloody young lamb'.

Walter Mansell and Uncle Albert took a load of stuff to Babel for the mutton-bird season. They got out to Babel on a dark, moonlit night and Uncle Albert said he would jump on to the rock, or what he thought was a rock. He fell in the water which was over his head. When he came up, Walter asked him for a match, to light his cigarette.

When Sir Harry Barron was over with the children on Cape Barren, Jim Boy Maynard then a small boy, was standing behind Sir Harry. Sir Harry Barron trod on Jim Boy's toe, 'Sorry, son' said Sir Harry. 'You're welcome, Sir', said Jim Boy.

Great-grandfather Harry Armstrong was coming down the road in the horse and cart when he saw a man running across a paddock with his trousers down, the man yelled, 'I can't help it if there's any women folk in the cart, because there's bull ants in me pants'.

Uncle Tas Smith went around his snares on a Good Friday. The snares were footies, so the wallabies were still alive. He was going to kill them but being Good Friday he let them go. On his way home he killed two snakes.

The Cape Barren Football Song (tune: 'Twenty-one years'):

*Come Whitemark footballers
And show us how to play.
The boys at Cape Barren
Will not run away.
There's most of your players
From Tassie or Vic.
The boys in our team
Can show them a trick,
At kicking and marking
And going up to
Stan, Hector and Keogh and Don Brownie too.*

*He favours his own team and that makes us mad
The last time we played he umpired bad.
Now we have an umpire with eyes sharp and keen.
He's only a sailor from out of the 'Jean'.
His name is Jack Lawson, a fair and just man.
So play up old Whitemark and win if you can.
You promised to play us three Saturdays past
But now you've arrived here to play us at last.
We'll soon start the game boys when the bell chimes
For we have been waiting a mighty long time.*

This song, Old Carren Crow, is by Grandfather Neuto Everett:

> The old carren crow
> Flew up the chimney
> And he won't come down.
> Begorra, if he don't I'll shoot him in the bum
> Old crow went quark, quark.
> (Chorus)
> Fall the diddle die doe
> Fall the diddle doe
> Fall the diddle die doe
> Fall the diddle doe

An Irish jig:

> Tiddy taddie, tiddy taddie, nine pound ten
> Tiddy taddie, tiddy taddie, nine pound ten

Grandfather Neuto was dancing the clog—tap dancing on a butter box. He said, 'I can't dance on this thing. It's too bloody slippery'. He was speaking to a parson.

He used to sing:

> The old grey badger
> Came down to the sea.
> I won't have him.
> I gave him some cheese that made him sneeze,
> And his old grey noodle shaking.
> The old grey badger
> Came down to the sea
> I won't have him.
> I gave him butter that made him stutter
> And his old grey noodle shaking.

This is a song about Dover:

> Sea, sea, sea, why are you angry with me.
> Ever since I left Dover, I thought the boat would go over.
> Oh, dear me, little Mary's been troubling me.
> When I reach the shore, I will say, 'Au revoir' to the sea, sea, sea.

We used to sing this song to a square dance:

> Oky, poky, finky fum,
> Poke your finger where
> You can't poke your thumb.

Polka:

> Run for the doctor
> Quick, quick, quick.

Clog:

> Gum boil, the belly ache,
> A pain in the big toe,
> A pimple on the chin.

All the children used to sing this one:

> Poor old so and so is dead.
> He fell through a hole in his bed.
> They put him in a coffin and he fell
> Through the bottom.
> Poor old so and so is dead.

Mulligan:

> Dyna and Mulligan went fishing for flies.
> Dyna gave Mulligan a pair of black eyes.
> Dyna said to Mulligan do you want anymore.
> No thank you said Mulligan
> My eyes are too sore.

There was also this one:

> Five boxes of matches and a pint of kerosine,
> A couple of plugs of dynamite and
> Then you ought to see.

SAYINGS

Uncle Tom Armstrong was a very slow man but when he did a job it was a good job. He used to walk with his arms behind his back, and when someone tapped him on the shoulder he would say 'tum tink'.

We had a lot of men called Ben. There was Long Beach Ben, Red Ben, Expecting a letter Ben, Black Ben and Mouth organ Ben.

PREMONITIONS

My mother always got premonitions and she was always right. Early one morning Mum came down to Gran' Aunt Millie and Uncle Johnnie Smith's at Brimworth. They had the phone on. We started to walk the miles to see them when Mum said there was something wrong. We wanted to know what it was and Mum said she could hear the organ playing a sad hymn. So we went down there. Gran' Aunt gave Mum a drink of tea, then the phone rang. Gran' Aunt said, 'Ivy, there is bad news. Your sister, Myrtle, passed away this morning'. Mum always said, 'What time did they pass away?' Mum always looked at the clock. My mother would say her prayers and say, 'Amen, Nee Nay', which means 'To you'.

Fanny Cochrane used to have premonitions too. Fanny would walk miles to find out what it was about. They said Fanny was always right, if any of her people passed away or they were very sick.

My brother-in-law, Arty West, saw his Aunty flying past him when he was out riding way out past Lady Barron on Flinders Island down Yellow Beach way. He was very scared and his horse galloped all the way home. Arty told his mother, and his father. They didn't believe him. He told them that he saw his Aunty flying past him with wings and he was only a child. The next day his father got up and saw the horse at the gate all of a lather. She had galloped round all night. They believed Arty then and they had to dry the horse down and put a rug over her. Young Arty was his Aunty Ella's favourite. She died sometime after he saw her flying past. When the news came down they always looked to see what time it was. They always looked at the clock. If you had a clock near by when the person died, they always asked, 'what time is it?'

My cousin Andrew Maynard had a boat called the *Evaline*. Vern Green, his nephew, worked with him and they had a load of guano on board, taking it from Cape Barren to Launceston. They had put too much aboard and that meant that the boat was low in the water. There was a bit of a swell and Andrew asked Vern to fix things on deck because it was rough. Andrew was worried about the load, and when he looked up at Vern he saw the Saviour laying across the deck. When Vern reached where the Saviour was laying he stepped over him each time he went back and forth on deck. Andrew could see all this happening but didn't tell Vern. The Saviour lay there until they got through the heads of the Tamar River in Launceston. Then the vision vanished and Andrew decided that the Saviour was there for a reason. He decided then that he would never overload the boat again.

Well, there was lots of other stories. I can't always think of what people used to do, what they used to see. There was a haunted house at Low Head. The story goes they sent two policemen there to see whether there was a woman screaming but they didn't hear anything. I don't think it was blowing—they only heard it when the wind was blowing a certain way. They sat up all night and, when they left at daylight, when they went to shut the door, one policeman got his overcoat caught in the door. He dropped it, so they reckon the house was haunted. They reckon it was built on top of a tree, and the tree was groaning underneath and that is why, with certain winds it screeched and made a row.

A man made his bed down on a grave but didn't know the grave was there until something told him that he was asleep on a grave. He knew someone was buried around there but he forgot where it was. He just shifted over then and went to sleep.

BIG SLAUGHTER

At the settlement on Flinders Island where Robinson took the Aborigines, some old one made wings to fly back. They were flogged. There's a terrible feeling there. The Holy Spirit is still there.

A house which was built there has stories about it. Mr Ralph Morton lived there years later. My father and Ralph Morton weren't frightened of anything. The Big Slaughter was at midnight. There was one room, a clock struck at midnight, it was every year at a certain time, shearing time or before the lambs were born. A youth went with Dad and Ralph Morton shearing. One night the dogs started howling and Ted covered his head up under the blankets. Dad said to him, 'What are you covering your head up for?' He said, 'The ghosts are coming', and then the clock struck midnight. There wasn't a clock in the house. As the years have gone by it seems as though justice has been done. Aboriginal people feel that the evil spirit, which was there, is now at rest. As things are being done to upgrade Wybalenna the evilness has gone but it is not forgotten. On Gun Carriage Island it is the same. There is a bank near a gully where, at a certain time just before dark, if you were using a plough, the horses would not go over that way. You could whip them but they still wouldn't go, that was the place of another bloody slaughter. Some very bad things have happened at Port Arthur, in the Midlands, and at Cape Grim.

VOICES

Ky Maynard and I used to go for a ride in the late afternoons. One day we went up to the corner of the road to Tanners Bay when we heard a grinding noise and people singing. We knew that it was voices, but couldn't understand them. Although we were frightened, we stopped to listen. The sound of the voices floated through the air down the Tanners Bay Road, and then we could see Uncle Johny Maynard, Ruby and Phillip driving the horse and sledge. They were singing 'Will the Angels Play their Harps For Me' and the grinding noise was the sledge on the gravel. We were so relieved as Tanners Bay was supposed to be haunted.

LUCY BEETON

Great-Grand-Aunt Lucy of Badger Island was the daughter of James Beeton and Emmerenna, an Aborigine. She was born on 14 May 1829. She was a big woman, clever and versatile. She was taught to sail boats by her father and she sailed to Launceston and between Chappell, Cape Barren and Flinders Islands and many other of the smaller islands. She carried sheep, grass tree gum and wood.

Miss Lucy Beeton, my great grand aunt.

When her nieces and nephews were born Lucy put in a great deal of time with her favourite niece, Isbella. Isbella's friends called her Miss Bella and her relations later called her Aunty Bella. The Reverend Brammall always called Lucy, Miss Lucy Beeton. When she was young Lucy was taught by private school teachers.

Lucy lived on Badger Island which is low and flat, a place where sheep and cattle graze. In the old days when a sheep was slaughtered the meat would be evenly distributed among all the island's inhabitants. Isbella Beeton lived on Badger after Lucy died in 1886. Neither she nor her two sisters had any children. Harriet married Jo Maynard and Mary married Alexander Maynard. They were both big women too and they always had plenty to eat.

The old home on Badger Island had a verandah with a grape vine growing around it. Inside there were many beautiful ornaments and pieces of furniture, including a piano. The women were often alone on the island and one night they didn't have a blind up to the kitchen window. One of them heard a voice saying, 'Don't look out the window'. Of course, she didn't but the next night there was a sheet up to that window. Those women had to be very brave.

Both Lucy and Bella reared a number of children.

Great-great-grandfather Beeton might have been a viscount for it has been said that he received money from England or through a merchant in Launceston. His wife, Emmerenna, used to have dresses sent to her from England but when great-great-grandfather died a relation of his wrote from England asking for her photograph. After she sent it she received no more clothes. This story was told to me by Dad, Uncle Bun and Gran' Aunt Milly Smith.

Lucy Beeton sometimes cooked doughnuts. It was always nice to see her old hands making the doughnuts. After being on the bird islands for a few days she would save the fat from the young birds, then render it in a camp oven, called a 'baker'. She would strain the fat to make sure it was clean, then take a five of plain flour, add a teaspoon of bi-carbonate of soda and two teaspoons of cream of tartar. She rubbed the cold fat into the dry mixture until it reached the right texture. Then she'd turn the mixture onto the table, rolled the dough flat and cut it into squares. Finally she would put them into the very hot fat in the camp oven, which was already hung over the fire. It was good to watch the frying doughnuts swirling around in the fat. They would puff up and turn a lovely golden brown. Lucy would put them on a dish to cool and later she'd split them open and fill them with jam. A meal fit for any queen.

James Beeton, brother of Lucy.

Chapter five
Nowadays

INVOLVEMENT IN THE COMMUNITY

I have been President of the Tasmanian Aboriginal Centre. I have also been involved in many other areas, one of them being fund raising in Burnie, Devonport, Launceston and Hobart. Many of our women made jam, pickles, relish and cakes. We also sold second hand clothes and books. We have got an arts and craft shop, and we are selling a few things, mainly from the mainland. There's a long way to go yet. We've got to make more Tasmanian things, which I think we can. I have travelled by train from Burnie to Hobart, over a hundred miles [160 kilometres], to take part in many activities in the Aboriginal community, including helping to raise funds for our Aboriginal children, for they are our future.

When I lived at Burnie the Brown boys came and asked me to join in the activities to form a branch of the Aboriginal Information Service on the north-west coast. I didn't really know what I was going for, but I soon learnt as I went around with my daughter gathering information. It wasn't an easy job, knocking at doors and asking who had dark blood in them, but on the whole they were all very good. We had to go right down to Queenstown, up the west-coast and the north-west. They all helped us as much as they could, but it wasn't very easy just the same to knock on the

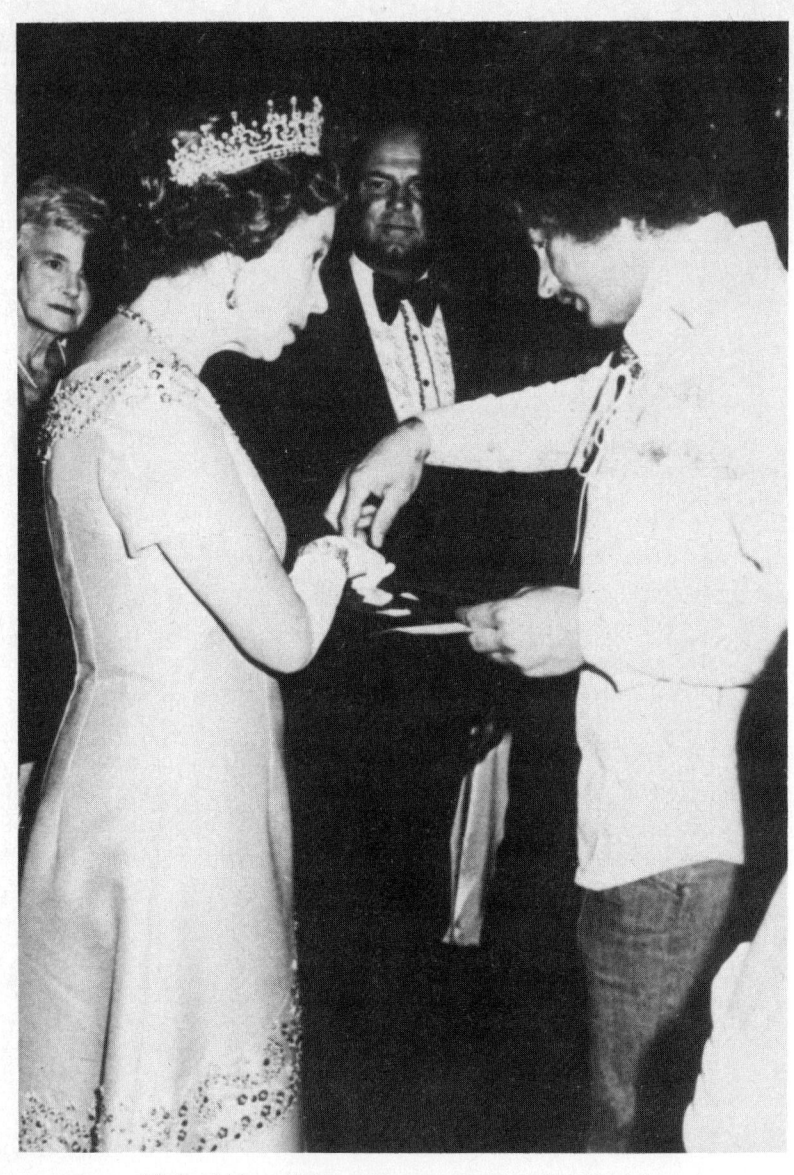

Michael Mansell presenting a petition to the Queen at Wrest Point in 1977.

door and ask them have they got a dab with the tar brush. Then we had to go to work, to form the north-west coast branch. We had a good little branch, but we had to make money, and we were a great force. Some of the shopkeepers were very good as far as donating things to raffle.

We had to sell Aborigine badges in the street, and in all my years I had never ever sold a ticket. Another lady and I were on the corner, then I thought, well, I've been helping white people to sell tickets, buying tickets that white people sell, so its the other way around this time. It was all right when we got started. I often help out the Salvation Army and one of their members came along and gave me a donation. The RSL club was very good, too.

We ran stalls in the Devonport main street. Then when we got used to it, we had stalls at Glenorchy (where I live now) to help the Aboriginal children at Christmas. Some of the children have parents with drink problems and when its all said and done little children can't help it.

Since I started at the TAC I think Aborigines have been made to feel they are somebody. They didn't feel that before because they were called half-castes, you might just as well say 'outcast'. I would like to thank Mr Mick Mansell for he called us Aborigines instead of using those words 'half-cast', and 'quarter-cast'. Terrible words. We know that we are someone of Aboriginal descent. It makes us feel a lot better, makes us feel that we're all someone.

One morning I was listening to radio 7ZR and I heard a man speaking about Alice Springs and the Aboriginal radio station there. I listened to some and it was lovely I just hope that it will be a success, because their music was lovely and the girl, I think it was, spoke beautifully. I just hope that it will go through all right and that they learn all they can. These people should have been educated years ago. It should have begun after Captain Cook landed in Botany Bay, not wait until all these years have passed.

CREMATION OF TRUGANINI

On the 30th April, 1976 a service was held at the Cornelian Bay Crematorium for Truganini. It was a closed service, the only people in attendance inside the chapel were the Premier, Mr Doug

Lowe, Dr Allan Wallace, Roy Nichols, the State Secretary of the Aboriginal Information Service, and other members of the Aboriginal community.

The skeleton of Truganini was viewed by the assembly and identified by Dr Wallace who pointed out various things which were related to Truganini's recorded history, e.g. missing finger, height, broken right forearm, etc. The coffin was carried by Mr Roy Nichols and Mr Lowe to the furnace—placed in and Mr Nichols and Mr Lowe waited until cremation had taken place. Under police guard the ashes were taken for safe keeping till the morning of 1st May, 1976 (100 years after her death). The ashes were contained in a Huon Pine casket which was placed in the *Egeria*'s cabin and carried to a point south-east of the pilot station in the D'Entrecasteaux Channel. Mr Lowe formally handed the ashes to Mr Nichols and the following words were said, 'Truganini, may you now rest in peace'.

Morgan Mansell presenting a wreath for the cremation of Truganini's bones.

On the *Egeria* were Mr Lowe, Roy Nichols, members of the Aboriginal community and a police guard. A flotilla of craft accompanied us down the river with cameras etc. Photographs were not allowed to be taken on board the *Egeria*, or during the service—because of the occasion. It was a solemn affair—giving this important person a decent and dignified burial.

Truganini's ashes were scattered on a lovely sunny morning about 10.30, a porpoise was swimming around us when the ashes went down. Truganini had asked for this to be done, but it took a hundred years to come about. My daughter Lenna and another lady were with the casket of Truganini before the cremation. Roslyn Langford made a speech at the cremation and it was very good.

Verna Nichols and her sister, Leonie Dickson, my nieces, are great-granddaughters of the Purdons who built the boat that took us all down the channel.

On 9 May people from the Aboriginal community and myself all went up to open a park which was dedicated to Truganini. It is called Truganini Park. The park is on the top of Mount Nelson which was used as a signal station years ago.

Mr Stephen Walker, a sculptor, made the commemorative plaque for the area which he set into a large stone and it looks lovely.

Guest speakers were Mr Doug Lowe, Roy Nichols, and Mr Bingham.

We had some little children sitting on top of some rocks watching what was going on. My grand-nieces and nephews were sitting there too with a few white children. They had their arms around each other. We were all standing around while they gave their speeches, a big black dog was standing with us too.

Truganini speech

This is the speech given by Roy Nichols at the dedication of Truganini Park:

As the person chosen by the Aboriginal people to represent them at this dedication, I have conflicting thoughts and emotions; a deep sadness, some hope for the future. The sadness comes from the past, the past that is Truganini: the destruction of a way of life, the tearing down of a set of values, the physical wiping out of a culture, Truganini typifies that destruction, in life and in death, and yet, out of all that, has come some cause for hope.

We the remnants of the Aboriginal people, the descendants of the race, now face, and look forward to the future with some cause, a reason for hope.

The dedication of this land today is not and cannot be the end, but marks a point: the end of one era, the beginning of another, because the real meaning of today's dedication must be its ongoing commitment not just from the government but also from the people. A commitment to ensure that the descendants of a race are allowed to escape from their oppression and live full lives within this society, whilst retaining their identity as descendants of the Aboriginal race. And I hope that this parkland itself will be regarded as an illustration of this ongoing commitment, a positive reminder to us all, that we cannot just bury the past as we have buried Truganini.

And in another way this ongoing commitment is expressed in the work of Stephen Walker for he did not just produce sculpture, a piece of design but regarded the wishes of the people as being an essential ingredient in his art form. He did not seek to go away by himself and create something which was just technically good, but as a true artist he took from us our hopes, our sadness, our dreams and our wishes and put them in his own form. He did not presume to know what our thoughts were. He asked us.

And yet what Stephen Walker has been able to do would not have been possible without the sense of responsibility and ongoing commitment of Doug Lowe, both as a minister of the Government and as a person who has shown a personal interest in the affairs of our people.

Why do I see cause for hope? Today is one of those causes. The gains that we have made at present are small, but they show the way. They show the way we are rediscovering our identity. They show they way because society at large is beginning to be aware of our identity and can only hope today will enable our search and our awareness to develop, so that the past that is Truganini, can merge into the future. That is our rightful heritage.

FANNY COCHRANE SMITH

Fanny Cochrane Smith was an Aboriginal lady, a very hard-working woman, who lived at Nicholls Rivulet. Fanny was taken in by a white family and was readily accepted by the white community. She married a William Smith on 2 October 1854 at the Independent Church in Hobart. They had eleven children. Fanny continued to press her claim that she, not Truganini, was the last of the full-bloods. She finally convinced Parliament, with the result that a resolution was passed in 1884 granting her land of two hundred acres in addition to the one hundred she already had at Port Cygnet. Fanny and William belonged to the Methodist Church. Fanny had a lovely singing voice. She recorded some songs two years before she died on 25 February 1905, at seventy-four. She had been in receipt of a Government annuity of 50 pounds a year and after her death she left her property to the Methodist Church. Her descendants still live in the same area. Fanny also got premonitions.

FAMILY AND THOUGHTS

I would like to thank people for what they all did to try and help me through over many years, and to thank the Aborigines too for what they have done. It's not easy doing the research, going asking questions here and there, and things are much harder now than they were about five years ago. It all costs more, too. I'm getting older and can't walk very far, or have a sleep on the grass floor like we used to do years ago. We would boil our billy on the fire and cook our Irish stews in the camp oven, boil our potatoes in their jackets. Still, I'll try to keep going.

This book has been written for the sake of the young ones. They still call it 'Aunty Ida's book'. Thank you to all the people who work at the Institute of Aboriginal Studies. This job has been keeping me going too.

I like to get up to Truganini Park when the weather is warm. It's nice to go up there and say a prayer and look down the Derwent River. There I feel something on the spiritual side, and I always feel better when I come back home again. Sometimes I wonder why that park is not used more often—it's not far out of

Hobart. I went up there one day and met a couple sitting around a seat. I went over and spoke to them. They were from Canada and they reckoned they couldn't understand why it wasn't used more. Its a lovely view when you get on the other side, and look down the Derwent river and remembering the past.

Leonie Dickson, my niece, has helped a lot too. After she worked at Fitzgerald's in Hobart for a long time she got married, and then she went to the Aboriginal Centre as a field officer. Roy Nichols was there as State Secretary and Leonie was field officer for a long time. I should think she would be one of the best field officers for down south that we've ever had. It's not an easy job but she seemed to always understand the people. You get a lot of insults but she seemed to battle it through.

My sister, Girlie, does a lot. She's very clever with her shell work. My other sister, Esma, collects all kinds of stamps, and she crochets and knits. I had another niece, Ann, who was a field officer at the TAC. Another nephew, Ralph Purdon, on Flinders Island, is learning a lot about our people. He's always loved to drive bulldozers and he clears land. He has his skipper's licence for a fishing boat as well. He is very strong, always likes to be where the roughest kind of work is, that's where Ralph likes to be.

It wasn't easy, for me, trying to rear a family without any help. I wasn't very clever, an old sadie with a mop and a broom cleaning out government offices, schools and the Marine Board. I liked my job as cleaner. It wasn't a very good job but at least I was trusted with keys. It was nice to know that people think you're honest enough to hold a key. I didn't get much money in those days, but I liked my bosses.

My nephew Lionel Reynolds can read the Bible inside out, and we need someone in Tasmania who can do this, because you can teach anyone a thing or two about race relations with a Bible. A Church leader came over from Sydney to hold a conference in Launceston, and this leader said something about the dark people. Lionel just got his Bible and walked straight up to where the leader was standing and told him a thing or two. He never ever went back to that church again.

My other niece Merle Reynolds, is the best raffle-ticket seller this side of the black stump. She could sell a Labor ticket to a

My daughter-in-law Elizabeth with grandchildren Mark, Wendy and Sally.

My grandson Robert Page and niece Verna Nichols.

Liberal. She works for Meals-on-wheels and and she takes out raffle books for the Aboriginal people.

My grand-children Mark, Wendy and Sally West also my grand-nieces and Nephew Kylie Dickson, Tanya and Jacqueline Langdon and John Dickson, are all very interested in sporting activities.

My other grandson, Robert Page, loves surfing and motor bikes, and is in his last year of apprenticeship as a fitter and turner.

My three grand-nieces on Flinders Island are also very keen sportsgirls, Joanne, Christine and Tracy Purdon. Verna Nichols, my niece, went to Albeura Street School and then on to Elizabeth Street High. Verna is a trained mothercraft nurse. She plays the organ and is good at oil painting. She went to work at the Aboriginal Centre as a secretary and later was the State Secretary. She also worked with her husband Roy Nichols on their forty-four foot fishing boat. When Roy was elected to the NAC she went to work for him as his secretary. She has also been very active in the Aboriginal community. Andrea Reynolds, my grand-niece, is very musical, and plays the organ just like her great-great grandmother Ivy Armstrong used to do.

All these children in their own way are active in the Aboriginal community and identify as Aboriginals.

Appendix one

This verse was told by Auntie Sarah Mansell.

In time to come
There will be no white man
There will be no black man
They will all be one.

Grand Uncle Johnny Smith's mother, known as Mother Brown. (Aboriginal name: Pleenperrnner.)

Appendix two

The Last of the Tasmanians by James Bonwick published in 1869 by Sampson Low, Son and Marston, London.

I read Mr Bonwick's book, and to me its the only accurate book about the history of the Aboriginal people.

I and everyone I knew was told what happened at the Settlement on Flinders Island. We were told that the Aborigines were put into a big grave. Probably only half of them were put there; the others were not there at all. They were sold. It doesn't matter what George Augustus Robinson puts on paper, or what they find of Robinson's. How do they know that it is the truth? My grandfather and other people have told us the story. They say that my great-great-grandfather, James Everett, killed his first wife or his mistress in the early days. I am supposed to come from that line. But apparently he never had any children, so somewhere along the way someone is wrong. People say that he murdered her, but it doesn't occur to them that she may have died of some disease, or that perhaps she was killed in self-defence.

As far back as I can remember there have always been hunters around and people snaring. When strangers came they always had to leave their gun at the garden gate or down the road a bit. They were not allowed to bring them near the home. Each person would go out and tell them to leave their gun or see that it wasn't loaded.

I can remember grandma Smith and my father saying that his mother and father and their families had beautiful things. The whole family had pictures and ornaments that came out from England. A lot of people of the present day think that they were all just wild people. But my people will still have the spiritual feeling, and people will still know what was done at places like the Settlement on Flinders Island, Gun Carriage Island, Cape Grim and Oyster Cove. It's still there and someone will walk over the graves and know the spiritual feeling.

Grand Aunt Elizabeth Everett who lived on Chappell Island.

George Everett, my great grandfather—brother to Elizabeth and son of James Everett.

    Our Lord, the same as your Lord probably, had to let them go the first round, but the next round he will be on our side. It's going that way now. He still loves us and we still love him. We know that he is there and we still believe in our God. I was always brought up to call people Mr and Mrs or Aunty or Uncle. It didn't make

Aunt Emma Maynard, midwife.

any difference whether they were our Aunt or Uncle. I had to respect my elders and it didn't matter which colour they were.

Most of my people disliked what was told to them about George Augustus Robinson and yet they liked Sir Harry Barron and Bishop Montgomery. Mr Knight, the school teacher on Cape Barren Island and Mrs Knight were loved very much. My Uncle had Mr Bonwick's book, the first one that came out, and he wrote in it, 'This was sad, it made your heart ache'. There was blood spilt everywhere. The first blood drawn by Europeans occurred when the first French navigator to come to Tasmania, Marion du Fresne, paid a visit to Frederick Henry Bay. The story is told by the French author, Domeny de Rienzi.

The following extracts are from James Bonwick's book.

"About an hour after the French landed, Captain Marion landed. Advancing in front of him, one of the Aborigines offered him a lighted firebrand, that he might set light to a heap of wood heaped on the flat shore. Marion took it, believing that it was a formality intended to give confidence to the savages; but hardly had the little pile of wood been enflamed, when the Aborigines retired in mass toward a little height, from which they threw afterwards a volley of stones, which wounded the two captains. They (the French) repelled them by several discharges of musket. They killed one aborigine and wounded several others, and the others fled howling towards the woods."

From another historian of the voyage we learn other particulars. A party of thirty Natives came down, the women carrying their children behind their backs, fastened on with ropes of rushes. The men were said to be carrying pointed sticks (spears) and stone axes. Presents of pieces of iron, looking-glasses, handkerchiefs, &c, were laid before them, but were rejected with sulky disdain. Some ducks and geese were tendered, but were angrily thrown back again. The fire-stick was presented to a sailor first, and afterwards to the captain. But evidently the act, supposed to be friendly, was taken in another spirit. They might have regarded it as a proof that the strangers intended an establishment upon their own hunting-grounds. The historian adds: "This was no sooner done, than they retired precipitately to a small hill, and threw a shower of stones, by which Captain Marion and the commander of the 'Castries' were both wounded." Shots, of course, replied to the stones, and the Frenchmen returned to their boats. Sending their women backward to the covert of the forest, the wild men ran along the shore after their foes. The sailors put back towards the land to arrest the pursuit. At this moment an old chief assumed the leadership, and raised a hideous war-cry, when a storm of spears answered to his call. Fifteen Frenchmen now chased the assailants, and by their destructive fire killed and wounded several of them.

The unfortunate Marion met with his death in New Zealand. Though a French author describes his countrymen as being fattened for thirty-two days, to be eaten on the thirty-third, yet it is known that the

New Zealanders treated them well till they polluted their sacred places, cooked food with tapued wood, and put two chiefs in irons. May they not have conducted themselves as ill in Tasmania, so as to incur the displeasure of the natives, and neglected to note the circumstance in their journal?

Captain Furneaux, of the 'Resolution', having got separated from his commander, Captain Cook, found himself off the south of Van Diemen's Land, in March 1773. Want of curiosity or opportunity gave him no tale to tell of the people in person, though he gathered some information of the country. Examining, on Bruni Island, a deserted 'wigwam', as he called a 'breakwind', he found a stone; he thereupon jumped to the conclusion that the Tasmanians, like the Fuegians, used a stone with tinder of bark for obtaining fire. He supposed them ignorant of metals and left in the hut nails, gun-flints, medals, and an old barrel. There could not be a large population, he thought, as he found but three or four huts in one place. Observing no evidence of the use of any appliances of civilization, he regarded the Natives, as he said, "altogether, from what we could judge, a very ignorant and wretched sort of people, though natives of a country capable of producing every necessary of life, and a climate the finest in the world." (pp. 3–4)

Captain Philip King, R.N., to whom Australia owes so much for the discovery or survey of the northern coast, has left us a short record of his experience of our islanders in 1819. Although after the settlement of Hobart Town, the visit was to a people who were strangers to men of our colour, and who lived on the stormy west coast.

"Our party," said he, "were amicably received by a tribe of Natives, consisting of six men and four old women; they came forward unarmed, but, as we afterwards found, their spears were concealed close at hand. Some presents were distributed amongst them, of which the most valuable, in their estimation, were empty wine bottles, which they called 'moke'. This word was, however, used by them for water only, so that it was doubtful whether the word meant the article itself, or the vessel that contained it. Our familiarity increased so rapidly, that by the time we had dug two wells to receive the water which was flowing over the beach they had become very inquisitive, and made no hesitation in searching our pockets and asking for everything they saw. One of the men, upon being detected in the act of pilfering a piece of white paper from Mr Cunningham's specimen box, immediately dropped it and drew back, much alarmed for fear of punishment, and also ashamed of having been discovered; but after a few angry looks from us the paper was given to him, and peace was soon restored. Our dog, being an object of much alarm, was fastened to the stern of our boat; a circumstance which prevented their curiosity from extending itself in that direction, and thus our arms were kept in convenient readiness without their knowledge. As soon as our boats were loaded and we had embarked, the Natives retired to the Bush, behind which we observed the heads of several children and young women. As many as sixteen were counted; so that this tribe, or family, might be composed of from twenty-five to thirty persons, of which we only saw six who were grown men. They were stouter and better proportioned than the Natives of New South Wales, and unlike them the hair was woolly; the only covering in use among them was a kangaroo skin, which they wore as a cloak over their shoulders."

The calmness and serenity of that year were changed into storm and disquietude in 1819.

It is the ever told tale of provocation and revenge. Early in the month of March the Oyster Bay tribe speared John Kemp and another man. But the journal of the day gives the provoking cause in these words: "It is well known that some time before Kemp was killed a native man was shot in the woods by some of the stockmen to the eastward, and that the women have been also deprived of their children in that quarter."

Where the Whites had no settlement the Blacks were found without the hostility of other places. Mr Kelly, the pilot, on discovering the spacious Macquarie Harbour, on the west coast, was pleased with the frank and manly attitude of the Natives. A letter addressed by a Hobart Town gentleman, in 1819, was published in the 'Asiatic Journal' of Calcutta the following year, and expresses the same opinion. "Several interviews," says the writer, "have lately taken place between the people of the settlement and the Natives of the west coast; who, as appears very probable, are debarred from all intercourse and interchange of sentiment with their countrymen on the eastern side, by that lofty range of mountains which intersects the island from the northern to the southern extremity. From the fearless and unsuspicious deportment of the former in these interviews, it would seem that the hostile disposition of the latter towards the people of the settlement was rather provoked by bad treatment than the spontaneous effect of their native ferocity." (pp. 48–50)

Governor Arthur was equally shocked at the barbarity of his people, and unable to prevent the evil. Immediately after his arrival in the colony, a tribe applied to him for protection, and it was readily granted. All that personal attention and kindness could do was done to retain them near Hobart Town, and to secure them from insult and injury. They settled at Kangaroo Point, a tongue of land separated from the town by the broad estuary of the Derwent. There they stayed quietly and happily for a couple of years, when a savage murder was committed by some of their white neighbours, and the camp broke up immediately for the haunts of wildness.

The infamous treatment of the poor females was the exciting cause of the bitter and revengeful spirit manifested by the Blacks toward our race. It was not alone that these unfortunates were the victims of their lust, but the objects of their barbarity. If perchance a woman was decoyed to the shepherd's hut, no gentleness of usage was employed to win her regard, and secure her stay; theatening language, the lash, and the chain were the harsher expedients of his savage love. A story is told by Dr Ross describing his journey up to the Shannon in 1823. "We met," said he, "one of Mr Lord's men sitting on the stump of a tree, nearly starved to death. He told us that three days before, a black woman whom he had caught, and had chained to a log with a bullock-chain, and whom he had dressed with a fine linen shirt (the only one he had), in hopes, as he said, to tame her, had contrived somehow to slip the chain from her leg, and ran away, shirt and all." The doctor adds, "I fear his object in chaining the poor creature was not exactly pure and disinterested." The reader will not be surprised to hear that not long after this gentle lover was hanged from exercising his benevolence upon some of his own countrymen. We hear of another who, having caught an unhappy girl, sought to relieve her fears, or subdue her sulks, as it was termed, by first giving her a morning's flogging with a bullock-whip, and then fastening her to a tree near his hut until he returned in the evening. The same fellow was afterwards found speared to death at a water hole.

A settler of the Esk informed me that a neighbour of his, wanting a 'gin', asked him to accompany him on his Sabine expedition. He had heard that a woman had been seen with a small party on an island in the river, and was then on his way thither to seize her. He pointed exultingly to a bullock-chain which he carried, as the means of capture. I was struck with the criticism of an "Old Hand," a rough carter, but one who carried a kind heart beneath a bear's skin. We were talking of the former times, and of the cruelty practised upon the Blacks, especially in the stealing of their women. With no particular admiration for the dark people, some of whom had tried their spears upon his body, he had a sense of manliness within him, and thus expressed his opinion: "If a man was to run away with my wife, don't you think if I could fall in with him that I wouldn't crack his head for him? I would so."

Old Tom Ward, who was transported in 1818, and who gave me some striking records of the past, said that when up the country in 1820, the stock-keepers of Mr Stocker's, of Salt Pan Plains, were guilty of abominable conduct toward two Native women. These afterwards told their 'Coolies' or husbands, and the tribe surounded the hut, and killed two men out of the three. Instances are upon record of murders committed solely with the view of seizing upon the females of a Mob. A lady once told me of a man-servant of hers getting speared after offering some insult to a 'gin'. He narrowly escaped with his life, being long confined to the hut. Repeated cases were known of brutal stock-keepers and shepherds emasculating the males. Horror-stricken by tales of men such as these, the benevolent Mr Backhouse exclaimed, "They were of such a character, as to remove any wonder at the determination of these injured people to try to drive from their land a race of men, among whom were persons guilty of such deeds." (pp. 59–61)

A respectable colonist, lately deceased in Melbourne, naming many instances of cruelty to the Natives, assured me that he knew of two men who had boasted of killing thirty at one time. Mr Backhouse relates that one party, out after the Blacks, killed thirty in capturing eleven. Quamby's Bluff, an eastern spur of the great central highlands of the island, curling up with its crest as if torn by violence from the Tier, was so called from a poor hunted creature there falling upon his knees, and shrieking out, "Quamby, Quamby—mercy, mercy." A gentleman, many years a magistrate in these colonies, mentioned to me the death of a shepherd of his near the Macquarie River. Soon after a company of soldiers went in pursuit of the supposed murderers. Falling in with a tribe around their night fires, in a gully at the back of the river, they shot indiscriminately at the group. Many were slain, but no Government inquiry was made into the well-known circumstance. An eye-witness of a similar night attack has this description: "One man was shot; he sprang up, turned round like a whipping top, and fell dead. The party then went up to the fires, found a great number of waddies and spears, and an infant sprawling on the ground, which one of the party pitched into the fire." (p. 62)

No more illustrative proof of the manners of that dark era can be presented, than we find recorded in the history of Jorgenson, when out in 1826: "Two days after I saw Scott," says he, "a large tribe came down to Dr Thomson's hut, which was occupied by three assigned servants. These men struck a bargain with some of the Blacks for some of their women, and in return to give them some blankets and sugar. However, no sooner were the females on their way to join their tribe, than the servants sallied out, and deprived them of their ill-gotten store. The Aborigines, nearly one hundred in number, now exceedingly exasperated, surrounded the hut, and had certainly effected their revenge, either by burning down the hut, or otherwise killing the aggressors, had not the Bushranger Dunn came to their timely assistance. Being so disappointed, the Blacks, in the heat of resentment, fell in with poor aged Scott, and murdered him in a most barbarous manner." This Scott had heretofore been on the most friendly terms with the Natives, and his dreadful end will furnish the key to many apparently inexplicable murders of innocent people, even women and children, by the Aborigines, when the two races were afterwards in frequent collision. (pp. 62–3)

In July 1827, a man was killed by the Blacks up in the country, near the Western Tiers. He had been long familiar with the tribe, having lived among the Natives of New Holland for some years, but had incurred their displeasure at last. The neighbouring settlers gathered together for a chase after the criminals, and took revenge indeed for the death of one; for the 'Colonial Times' declares: "They report that there must be about sixty of them killed and wounded."

A party of the Richmond police were passing through the Bush in 1827, when a tribe, seeing them, got up on a hill and threw stones upon them. The others fired in return, and then charged them with the bayonet. We have Mr G A Robinson's authority for stating tht "a party of military and constables got a number of Natives between two perpendicular rocks, on a sort of shelf, and killed seventy of them, dragging the women and children from the crevices of the rocks, and dashing out their brains."

A wretched man, named Ibbens, was accustomed to go persistently after the Eastern tribe with a double-barrelled gun, creeping among them at dusk, until he had killed the half of them. One man boasted that he had thrown an old woman upon the fire, and burnt her to death. The 'Colonial Times' speaks on one occasion of a party of soldiers and others approaching within thirty yards of their night-fires, and killing "an immense quantity of the Blacks." Well might Dr Marshall tell Lord Glenelg, "The murders which, at almost every page, have blotted with blood the history of the British Colonies, cry out against us unto the Most High God, with a voice that has not always been unanswered, for national calamity to succeed national wickedness."

Many years ago I fell in with one of the lowest order of convicts, who assured me that he liked to kill a black fellow better than smoke his pipe;

adding, "and I am a rare one at that, too." He related the following adventure. Out one evening with some armed stock-keeping mates, he climbed Maloney's Sugar Loaf, and saw a tribe lighting their fires for the night. He returned with the news. Then, abstaining from noise and supper-fire themselves, they waited till just before dawn, advanced toward their unsuspicious victims in a crescent line, so as to cut off retreat, and fired close. He quietly remarked: "There wasn't many of them got off." I dissembled a little, and in an off-hand way inquired how many he had cleared off. He shook the stump of his amputated arm, smiled archly at me, and said, "No—no—that's not a fair question." (pp. 64–5)

My worthy friend a much respected Tasmanian colonist, is my authority for the story of a sad tragedy. Two men went out shooting birds. Some Natives, seeing them approach, hastily fled. A woman, far advanced in pregnancy, unable to run with the rest, climbed up a tree, and broke down the branches around her for concealment. But she had been observed by the sportsmen. One of these proposed to shoot her, but the other objected. The first, however, dropped behind, and fired at the unfortunate creature. A fearful scream was heard, and then a new-born infant fell out of the tree. That very day the wife and child of this monster were crossing the Derwent, when a sudden squall upset the boat, and both were drowned.

That gentleman also told me that, when young, a fellow gave him an account of some capital fun, as it was called. He and some others took advantage of a robbery at Hamilton, and charged it upon an inoffensive tribe in the neighbourhood. Without warning, an expedition was fitted out in the night, and a terrible slaughter took place. The miserable remnant were infuriated at the treachery and cruelty, and revenged themselves by years of outrage and murder.... [Someone's] father was dining with a country settler, when a man came in, and called out, "Well, Master! I've shot three more crows to-day,"—meaning, 'Blacks'. (pp. 65–6)

The cruelty took an indirect turn with some of these out-station people. Thus, Captain Holman talks about a fellow taking a pair of pistols, one only of which was loaded, and seeking to amuse a native by firing the harmless one at his own ear. Then, presenting the other weapon to the man, and inviting him to try the same funny performance on himself, he had the grim delight of seeing the black fellow's brains blown out.

Let us turn, for relief, to a pleasing story of 1822. A tribe had lighted their evening fires in the Bush not far from a field of corn ready to cut, and the flames were carried by a high wind toward the farm. The farmer writes: "We were doing our best to extinguish it by beating the flames out with green boughs, but our efforts would have been in vain had not the whole tribe of Blacks all at once come forward to assist me. Even some hours afterwards, when the flames again broke out in two or three places, they were on the alert in a moment to put them out. I mention this incident, as it was an act of friendship on their part, and shows that when they have not been insulted, or had cause of revenge, and are able to discriminate their friends from their foes, they are not wanting to reciprocate offices of friendship and humanity." (p. 67)

The 'Line', the most formidable part of the Black War, was formed towards the close of 1830. It was not like the celebrated 'Thin-Red Line' of the Crimea, seen and seeing all the way, but a 'cordon' of more unequal character, to drive the Aborigines into a corner of Tasmania.

History is not without parallels of a 'Line' operation. A 'levy en masse' for a similar purpose took place in Governor Macquarie's time. The Natives of New South Wales had been very troublesome; and, in 1816, General Macquarie summoned the colonists, with all available military and constabulary, and drove the Blacks before him beyond the Blue Mountains, with great slaughter. This may have suggested to the authorities of Van Diemen's Land the scheme eventually adopted there.

As has been stated, a remarkably hopeful Government paper appeared in August 1830, which urged the colonists not to hurt the well-disposed Natives, but rather give them a dinner, with smiles, and let them depart with a blessing. A reconsideration of the subject, after loud complaints of his people, induced Colonel Arthur to qualify his statement, and quiet the surges of public opinion. (p. 131)

The 'Three Thumbs' often appear before the eye of the reader of the 'Line' proceedings. It was a district of singular advantage to a beleaguered enemy. The three hills were about two hundred yards apart, and were covered to the summit with huge Eucalyptus trees, and a dense underwood, that made it almost wholly impervious to any but Natives. The surrounding scrub was seven miles long from east to west, and from two to four broad. It was situated half a dozen miles to the south-west of Prosser's Bay, and, therefore, not far from the Peninsula. This Malakoff of the foe must be stormed. As, according to the 'Courier's' Special Correspondent, "into this ambush the great body of the Blacks have embowered themselves," the place must be turned. To quote still from the Dr Russell of the period: "The difficulties in *accomplishing this are of course immense, but we trust not insurmountable, and the thing must be done."* (p. 168)

A hut near Jerusalem was robbed, and a poor woman speared to death. Fires began to redden the sky, and shrieks of terror told the tale of woe. A letter from Perth said that one hundred and fifty had burst through the 'Cordon', and were plundering to the rear of Major Gray's, at Avoca. Thirty were seen and chased by the intrepid John Batman, who was successful in securing a good part of them, and without bloodshed.

The Launceston papers were annoyed at the defenceless state of the north, and asked why all the effort of the colony should be directed, to the alarm and desertion of settlements, for the capture of two tribes—those of Oyster Bay and Big River—as if others were not as sanguinary elsewhere. (p. 169)

The work was over, and the labourers could leave the field. The Rev. Mr. West, in his 'History of Tasmania,' has expressively written: "The Settlers Soldiers returned to their homes, their shoes worn out, their garments tattered, their hair long and shaggy, with beards unshaven, their arms tarnished, but neither blood-stained nor disgraced." (p. 173)

The following extracts from James Bonwick's book refer to William Lanne.

A couple of months after Lanne went whaling again. He returned in the 'Runnymede' in February of the present year, bloated and unhealthy. For several days he complained of sickness. On the Friday he was suddenly seized with choleraic diarrhoea, and his system was unable to bear up against the attack. The following day he attempted to dress himself, with a view of proceeding to the hospital for treatment, but the exertion overcame him, and he fell dead on the bed. (p. 395)

As previously stated by us, the body had been removed from the Dog and Partridge Hotel, where the man died, to the dead-house at the Hospital, and, on an order being sought for its removal to the undertakers, it was declined, on the ground that, as the body was of the greatest scientific value, the authorities were determined to do all in their power to protect it. An application to the Colonial Secretary met with the same reply, and the Hon Sir Richard Dry sent positive instructions to Dr. Stokell that the body of "King Billy" should be protected from mutilation . . .

At that hour between fifty and sixty gentlemen presented themselves at the institution, and found all in readiness for the burial. Rumours had, meanwhile, got afloat to the effect that the body had been tampered with, and Captain McArthur, Mr Colvin, and some others interested in the deceased, from his connexion with the whaling trade, requested that the coffin should be opened, in order to satisfy their minds that the ceremony of burial was not altogether a "vain show." This was done by Mr Graves, and the body was seen by those who desired to see it, in the condition which will be hereafter described. The lid was then again screwed down, and, at the suggestion of some of those present, the coffin was sealed. (p. 396)

At the cemetery the Rev. Mr. Cox read the second portion of the impressive Burial Service of the English Church, and the grave closed over "King Billy," the breast-plate on whose coffin bore the simple inscription, "William Lanne, died March 3d, 1869. Aged 34 years." (p. 397)

Besides the Royal Society, it seems that there were others who desired to secure "Billy Lanne's" skeleton, and who were determined to have it in spite of the positive orders of the Colonial Secretary. The dead-house at the hospital was entered on Friday night, the head was skinned and the skull carried away, and with a view to conceal this proceeding, the head of a patient who had died in the hospital on the same day, or the day previously, was similarly tampered with, and the skull placed inside the scalp of the unfortunate native, the face being drawn over so as to have the appearance of completeness. On this mutilation being discovered, the members of the Council of the Royal Society were greatly annoyed, and feeling assured that the object of the party who had taken the skull was afterwards to take the body from the grave, and so possess himself of the perfect skeleton, it was resolved to take off the feet and hands and to lodge them in the Museum, an operation which was carefully done. The funeral then took place as above described.

It is believed, however, that the skull was thrown over the wall at the back of the dead-house with a string attached to it, and that it was secured by a confederate stationed in the creek on the other side. These reports occasioned a very painful impression among those present at the funeral, and a deputation consisting of Messrs. Colvin, McArthur, and Bayley, waited upon Sir Richard Dry in the evening, and requested that steps should be taken to have the grave watched during the night. Sir Richard at once acquiesced in the proposal, and instructions were given to the police, but in some way they miscarried, possibly owing to the fact that they were not communicated through his Worship the Mayor, and the consequence was that the grave was found disturbed yesterday morning, when Constable Mahony reported that the earth had been removed, that a skull had been found lying on the surface, that a part of the coffin was visible, and that the ground surrounding the grave was saturated with blood. During the morning this report spread through the city, and several hundreds of persons visited the cemetery in the afternoon. (p. 398–9)

It is sufficient to add that Dr Crowther was suspended as honorary surgeon of the hospital, that the skeleton was in possession of the Royal Society of Tasmania, and that, according to the 'Launceston Examiner', "it is expected that one of the first orders on the assembling of Parliament will be a 'return of King Billy's head'!" (p. 399)

In his memoirs Dr Crowther recalled a song popular in Hobart Town while the official enquiry was being held.

> *King Billy's dead*
> *Crowther had his head*
> *Stokell has his hands and feet*
>
> *My feet, my feet, my poor feet*
> *that used to be so gritty*
> *They're not aboard the Runnymede*
> *They're somewhere in this city*

Brunton Stephens said that the skull was to be found:

> *In a certain museum*
> *I won't say where*
> *but it's no very far*
> *from Russell Square*

The following poem is from J. Brunton Stephens (1880) *Miscellaneous Poems*, Watson, Ferguson, Brisbane.

> *King Billy's Skull*
> *Fancy the honour, the kudos, the fame*
> *A whole museum athrill with one's name*
> *Fancy the thousands all crowding to see*
> *the skull of the last aborigine*
> *Presented by *—M.D.*